Winning in the Job Market

For over twenty-five hundred years, *The Art of War* has helped readers find **competitive advantage** using the secrets of Sun Tzu.   In this adaptation, we apply these ancient secrets to building a career. As you will see, this book covers everything you need for a successful career:

- finding the best jobs
- getting hired
- dealing with organizational politics
- succeeding in your current position
- getting promoted
- moving to another organization.

This volume contains **two books.** It contains **the complete text** of Sun Tzu's *The Art of War*. It also contains a detailed, line-by-line adaptation called *The Art of Career Building.* This adaptation applies Sun Tzu's immortal words to creating a successful career in today's job market.

This book is only the beginning...

This book also contains **the secret password keys** that allow you to access *The Warrior Class*, the world's largest site for on-line training in Sun Tzu's methods (see **www.clearbridge.com** for information). This site contains hundreds of pages of training material to help you master Sun Tzu's techniques. This material is **FREE** to the owners of this book.

Buy this book today and study its ideas forever!

Other *Art of War* Works from Clearbridge Publishing

SUN TZU'S
THE ART OF WAR
plus
THE ART OF
CAREER BUILDING

孫
子
兵
法

To my brothers, Mark & Gregg

SUN TZU'S

THE ART OF WAR
plus
THE ART OF
CAREER BUILDING

BY
GARY GAGLIARDI

Published by
Clearbridge Publishing

Manufactured in the United States of America
Front Cover Art by Gary Gagliardi
Back Cover photograph by Rebecca Gagliardi

Library of Congress Control Number 2002090338
ISBN 1-929194-13-7
Clearbridge Publishing's books may be purchased for business, for promotional use, or for special sales. Please contact:

Clearbridge PUBLISHING
P.O. Box 33772, Shoreline, WA 98133
Phone: (206)-533-9357 Fax: (206)-546-9756
www.clearbridge.com
info@clearbridge.com

CONTENTS

How to Use This Book

This is a different type of book about careers. It won't tell you how to write a resume or handle an interview. Instead, it addresses the long-term, strategic issues of building a career. It is about choosing the right job, getting recognized and promoted in your jobs, and using one position as the stepping stone to new, better position. More importantly, as a guide to a career strategy, it directly adapts the world's best book on strategy, Sun Tzu's *The Art of War,* to the specific problem of building a career.

For over two thousand years, people have preserved and treasured Sun Tzu's famous treatise on war for one reason: its competitive methods work extremely well. As the first of the military classics, *The Art of War* offers a distinct, non-intuitive philosophy on how to discover a path. This philosophy works in any dynamic environment where people find themselves contesting with one another for a specific goal. This book on using Sun Tzu's methods for building a career grew directly our of our seminars on *The Art of War* where attendees asked specifically about how to apply Sun Tzu's methods to finding jobs, dealing with organizational politics, and so on.

In addressing the question about whether or not Sun Tzu's methods work in managing a career, I can only point to my own experience. Before I discovered *The Art of War*, I basically drifted from job to job. After I started studying and using Sun Tzu's methods, I was promoted on an average of every eight months. My job changes eventually putting me in the position of starting a successful software business that went on to become one of the Inc. 500 fastest growing, privately owned businesses in America.

In many cases, following Sun Tzu's philosophy is difficult. For example, when I made the move to get into the computer industry, I left a high-paying sales management job with BIC Pen to become a sales clerk in a Radio Shack computer store. It was years before I made the same salary I was making before the change. Fortunately, by choosing that path, I reached my goal of becoming financially independent. Sun Tzu's system is about finding the best path to long-term goals with minimal risk, and it may not produce the highest paying job at each step of the way.

This book offers the complete text of *The Art of War* plus a line-by-line adaptation applying Sun Tzu's lessons to the problems of career advancement. In reading *The Art of War* and *The Art of Career Building* side-by-side, I encourage you to think about your own problems in advancing your career and *make notes* about how to apply Sun Tzu's suggestions to your own situation. Sun Tzu's advice is very general because it was written to be applied to all types of competition.

Even in applying *The Art of War* specifically to advancing a career, you will draw different lessons from the text depending on your situation when you read it. For this reason, we recommend that in managing your career, you reread this book every six months or so to keep yourself on track.

Why should Sun Tzu's concept of warfare apply so well to the problems of managing a career? It works because all competition, including the competition for different jobs, arises from the same factors. Sun Tzu wrote about human nature, confrontation, and what matters in a contest of wills. The nature of competition has not changed in the last two thousand years and it will not over the next two thousand. The only differences between job competition and warfare are the types of tools we use and the nature of the battleground.

Sun Tzu realized that competition is, by nature, a chaotic system. He used the term "chaos" in a surprisingly modern, scientific sense. He did not mean that competitive systems do not have structure. He meant that they are complex, self-organizing systems from which patterns naturally emerge but in which specific events are very difficult to predict or control. Those who wish to understand the true nature of competition are well served studying modern chaos theory. If you do, you will discover that many of its principles were uncovered by Sun Tzu twenty-five hundred years ago.

People mistakenly see war—and, more generally, competition—as an adversarial, destructive process, but Sun Tzu saw it as a necessary component of a productive world. He saw competition as costly but not necessarily destructive. He was familiar with the potentially destructive nature of war, and he teaches us how to minimize the costs of competition through logic and persuasion. He teaches methods that avoid the most costly forms of conflict and yet allow us to win new positions and territory.

This approach works equally well to getting promotions and finding better jobs. From Sun Tzu, we learn how to discover new job positions, how to evaluate them, and how to win these positions with minimal risk. We learn how to plan moves from one position to the next, continually advancing our career.

As you read this book, notice how closely *The Art of Career Building* follows Sun Tzu's original ideas in *The Art of War*. While *The Art of Career Building* applies Sun Tzu's ideas in ways that he would never have foreseen, it does so respecting the integrity of his thinking. I truly don't think of these career advancement ideas as my own but rather as interpretations of

Sun Tzu's approach to successful competition. I follow his advice and admonitions as closely as possible, line-by-line.

When we adapt Sun Tzu's methods of warfare to career building, the lessons that emerge from Sun Tzu are intriguing. First, Sun Tzu teaches that winning a job is not enough. The goal is to win easily with minimal risk. The first step in finding a better job is doing well in our existing job. We never want to be in a position of looking for a new job because we are out of work. People who are out of work never get the best jobs unless they are in the process of creating their own company. We only want to fight for a position in situations where we are certain to win, but we also want to be certain that winning is well worth the cost. In most of the career-building adaptation, we do not discriminate between changing jobs within a company and finding a job in a different company. In Sun Tzu's system, both are competitive moves that must be carefully evaluated before they are undertaken.

Sun Tzu is specific about what to do in certain situations. He wants us to pay close attention to the details of our work situation. He enumerates different job conditions, different types of opponents, different potential decision-making mistakes, different competitive signals, and so on. Although Sun Tzu wrote 2,500 years ago about warfare, when translated to career building, his detailed lists are still surprisingly complete. His advice is useful to anyone planning their career.

Sun Tzu offers a "cooperative" view of competition. In his mind's eye, we cannot win through our own actions. We do not create our next job opportunity. We can perform in our existing job very well, but we discover new opportunities only when others create them. The secret is recognizing a good opportunity when it presents itself. A pay raise alone is not an opportunity. We must always be looking for broader, more important positions where we can solve someone's problem.

Finally, Sun Tzu's view of competition is knowledge-intensive. Sun Tzu sees victory going to the person who is the most knowledgeable. He even recognizes creativity as a special type of knowledge. In Sun Tzu, there is no substitute for good information. We are beginning to realize that people in the economy are paid for their knowledge, but knowledge in Sun Tzu's system is more than knowing what we need to do our job at the moment. It means learning our industry from top to bottom.

This version of *The Art of War* is just one of many versions and adaptations offered by Clearbridge Publishing. We provide or will provide adaptations for every common form of competition in modern life. We suggest you visit **www.clearbridge.com** for a complete list of our current titles.

For further in-depth study of Sun Tzu's methods, we have created *The Warrior Class*, our on-line training center, which contains hundreds of slides, text lessons, and tests to help people master Sun Tzu. Access to the on-line site is FREE to anyone buying any one of our books. See **www.clearbridge.com** for more information on accessing *The Warrior Class*.

Gary Gagliardi, 2002

PLANNING

This is war.
It is the most important skill in the nation.
It is the basis of life and death.
It is the philosophy of survival or destruction.
You must know it well.

Your skill comes from five factors.
Study these factors when you plan war.
You must insist on knowing the nature of:
1. military philosophy,
2. the weather,
3. the ground,
4. the commander,
5. and military methods.

It starts with your military philosophy.
Command your people in a way that gives them a higher
shared purpose.
You can lead them to death.
You can lead them to life.
They must never fear danger or dishonesty.

CAREER PLANNING

You must build your career.
It is the central focus of your professional life.
It is the foundation of prosperity or poverty.
It is the basis of progress or stagnation.
You must understand your career.

Five factors determine your professional success.
Evaluate these factors when planning your career.
You must know:
  (1) your career goals,
  (2) the trends in the job market,
  (3) your career options,
  (4) your job skills,
  (5) and your career building methods.

Career building begins with your career goals.
When you evaluate a job, you must look for more than just
a paycheck.
You must avoid wasting your energy.
You must make the most productive use of your time.
Your goals must safeguard your future.

3

Next, you have the weather.
It can be sunny or overcast.
It can be hot or cold.
It includes the timing of the seasons.

Next is the terrain.
It can be distant or near.
It can be difficult or easy.
It can be open or narrow.
It also determines your life or death.

Next is the commander.
He must be smart,
trustworthy,
caring,
brave,
and strict.

Finally, you have your military methods.
They include the shape of your organization.
This comes from your management philosophy.
You must master their use.

All five of these factors are critical.
As a commander, you must pay attention to them.
Understanding them brings victory.
Ignoring them means defeat.

Next are the trends in the job market.
The business climate can change from good to bad.
Certain jobs grow more important with time.
The trends in the job market will change with time.

Next are your career options.
You can stay with your company or change companies.
You can look for a challenge or something easy.
You can be wide open to options or be very selective.
Choosing the right path determines your success or failure.

Next are your job skills.
You must be knowledgeable,
honest,
people-oriented,
adventurous,
and disciplined.

Finally, you need a well-defined career building process.
It must include a network of business contacts.
Your methods arise naturally from your career goals.
You must get comfortable with looking for advancement.

All five of these factors are critical.
You must continuously evaluate them.
Your success depends on them.
Disregarding them leads to failure.

You must learn through planning.
You must question the situation.

You must ask:
Which government has the right philosophy?
Which commander has the skill?
Which season and place have the advantage?
Which method of command works?
Which group of forces has the strength?
Which officers and men have the training?
Which rewards and punishments make sense?
This tells when you will win and when you will lose.
Some commanders perform this analysis.
If you use these commanders, you will win.
Keep them.
Some commanders ignore this analysis.
If you use these commanders, you will lose.
Get rid of them.

Plan an advantage by listening.
This makes you powerful.
Get assistance from the outside.
Know the situation.
Then planning can creates advantages and controls power.

Career planning is a constant education.
You need to continually question your situation.

You must ask this:
Which opportunity is consistent with your goals?
Are you developing your job skills?
When and where should your career go?
Which career advancement techniques work best?
Which groups have control over your career?
Which opportunity gives you training for the future?
What risks and rewards make sense?
This analysis tells you where you can and cannot advance.
You must continually do such career analysis.
If plan your career, you will be successful.
Keep at it.
Most people never plan their career.
If you are one of them, you will go nowhere.
You must change.

☙—

Planning forces you to listen to other people.
Knowledge of the job market makes you powerful.
Get help from people outside your company.
Know your job situation.
Planning uncovers your strengths and directs your energies.

☙—

Warfare is one thing.
It is a philosophy of deception.

When you are ready, you try to appear incapacitated.
When active, you pretend inactivity.
When you are close to the enemy, you appear distant.
When far away, pretend you are near.

If the enemy has strong position, entice him away from it.
If the enemy is confused, be decisive.
If the enemy is solid, prepare against him.
If the enemy is strong, avoid him.
If the enemy is angry, frustrate him.
If the enemy is weak, make him arrogant.
If the enemy is relaxed, make him work.
If the enemy is united, break him apart.
Attack him when he is unprepared.
Leave when he least expects it.

You will find a place where you can win.
Don't pass it by.

Career building means one thing:
It means controlling people's perception of you.

If you are unprepared, you must appear prepared.
If you are working hard, you must make it look easy.
When close to making a move, appear willing to wait.
When no move is planned, appear ready for a change.

When a good position is available, court it.
When others are uncertain, be decisive.
When jobs get competitive, protect yourself.
When someone is entrenched, move around his position.
If the hiring decision is emotional, play to that emotion.
If your opposition is weak, make them overconfident.
If the decision-maker is relaxed, make him wake up.
If a job change requires agreement, line up supporters.
Go after positions that others have overlooked.
Leave a job when others least expected it.

You will often find a position that advances your career.
Never pass it by.

Before you go to war, you must believe that you can count
on victory.
You must calculate many advantages.
Before you go to battle, you may believe that you can foresee
defeat.
You can count few advantages.
Many advantages add up to victory.
Few advantages add up to defeat.
How can you know your advantages without analyzing them?
We can see where we are by means of our observations.
We can foresee our victory or defeat by planning.

Before going after a new job, you must know that you can win it.

You must know that you are the most qualified.

Before wasting your efforts, you must avoid jobs that you cannot win easily.

You must know when you do not have the qualifications.

Good qualifications add up to winning the position.

Poor qualifications add up to losing the position.

How can you build your qualification without planning?

You must know how well you are doing where you are.

You can control your advancement by planning.

GOING TO WAR

Everything depends on your use of military philosophy.
Moving the army requires thousands of vehicles.
These vehicles must be loaded thousands of times.
The army must carry a huge supply of arms.
You need ten thousand acres of grain.
This results in internal and external shortages.
Any army consumes resources like an invader.
It uses up glue and paint for wood.
It requires armor for its vehicles.
People complain about the waste of a vast amount of metal.
It will set you back when you raise tens of thousands of
troops.

Using a large army makes war very expensive to win.
Long delays create a dull army and sharp defeats.
Attacking enemy cities drains your forces.
Long campaigns that exhaust the nation's resources are
wrong.

Changing Jobs

Everything depends on your career goals.
Building a career requires thousands of decisions.
Building a career involves finding new positions.
You must develop a host of skills.
You must invest time and energy.
Career building takes time away from your family.
It can consume your life if you let it.
It requires creativity and imagination.
It demands that you perform your existing job well.
People will always complain about what they are paid.
You will fall behind in your career if you take a job simply because it pays more.

A big paycheck can make moving to the right job difficult.
Staying too long in the wrong job leads to failure.
Attacking an entrenched superior drains your energy.
A long period in a position that drains your momentum is wrong.

Manage a dull army.
You will suffer sharp defeats.
Drain your forces.
Your money will be used up.
Your rivals multiply as your army collapses and they will begin
against you.
It doesn't matter how smart you are.
You cannot get ahead by taking losses!

You hear of people going to war too quickly.
Still, you won't see a skilled war that lasts a long time.

You can fight a war for a long time or you can make your
nation strong.
You can't do both.

You can never totally understand all the dangers in using
arms.
Therefore, you can never totally understand the advantages in
using arms either.

You want to make good use of war.
Do not raise troops repeatedly.
Do not carry too many supplies.
Choose to be useful to your nation.
Feed off the enemy.
Make your army carry only the provisions it needs.

14

You can get stuck in the wrong job.
Then you will find yourself doing poorly.
It drains your energy.
The paycheck that holds you is soon gone.
As your enthusiasm fades, you inspire opponents to attack you.
It does not matter how smart you think you are.
You cannot get ahead once you have lost the initiative.

You can sometimes move between jobs too quickly.
However, the slower your progress, the more often you fail.

You can be lazy when you looking for a new position or you can be successful.
You can't have it both ways.

You can never completely insure against failure when you go into a new position.
Nor can you know all the opportunities of moving into a new position.

You must make good use of your existing position.
Do not repeatedly ask for raises.
Do not accumulate large debts.
Choose to be invaluable to your employer.
Generate money.
Spend only the money you absolutely must.

The nation impoverishes itself shipping to troops that are far
away.
Distant transportation is costly for hundreds of families.
Buying goods with the army nearby is also expensive.
These high prices also impoverish hundreds of families.
People quickly exhaust their resources supporting a military
force.
Military forces consume a nation's wealth entirely.
War leaves households in the former heart of the nation with
nothing.

War destroys hundreds of families.
Out of every ten families, war leaves only seven.
War empties the government's storehouses.
Broken armies will get rid of their horses.
They will throw down their armor, helmets, and arrows.
They will lose their swords and shields.
They will leave their wagons without oxen.
War will consume sixty percent of everything you have.

Because of this, the commander's duty is to feed off the
enemy.

Use a cup of the enemy's food.
It is worth twenty of your own.
Win a bushel of the enemy's feed.
It is worth twenty of your own.

You can kill the enemy and frustrate him as well.
Take the enemy's strength from him by stealing away his
supplies.

Relocating to a new city to win a new position is expensive.
Traveling to interview for a new position is costly.
Staying in a crowded job market is also expensive.
Staying in bad job markets impoverishes you.
You can quickly exhaust your bank account looking for work.
Employment agencies can consume your resources entirely.
Looking for work can impoverish your entire family and leave you with nothing.

The economy is risky.
Companies go out of business.
Competition pressures everyone in the job market.
People without jobs will take any position.
They are willing to work for low pay and benefits.
They do not worry about protecting themselves.
They lose their houses and cars.
Without work, people will lose most of what they have.

Because of this, your success comes from making your employer successful.

Take a dollar of pay in shared profits.
It is worth twenty dollars in salary.
Win bonuses based on your performance.
They are worth twenty times than guarantees.

You must be productive and indispensable.
You must generate much value in the business than your pay consumes.

Fight for the enemy's supply wagons.
Capture their supplies by using overwhelming force.
Reward the first who capture them.
Then change their banners and flags.
Mix them in with your own to increase your supply line.
Keep your soldiers strong by providing for them.
This is what it means to beat the enemy while you grow more
powerful.

Make victory in war pay for itself.
Avoid expensive, long campaigns.
The military commander's knowledge is the key.
It determines if the civilian officials can govern.
It determines if the nation's households are peaceful or a
danger to the state.

Fight for business for your employer.
Focus all your efforts on making your company a success.
Insist on being rewarded for your efforts.
Insist on being recognized for the business you've won.
Your company will be better able to support you.
Your job will be secure because you are needed.
This is what it means to win in competition while building your career.

Make your job search pay for itself.
Avoid staying in the same position for too long.
Your knowledge of your field is the key.
It determines your ability to manage your career.
It determines how valuable you are as an employee and how easily you can move up.

PLANNING AN ATTACK

Everyone relies on the arts of war.
A united nation is strong.
A divided nation is weak.
A united army is strong.
A divided army is weak.
A united force is strong.
A divided force is weak.
United men are strong.
Divided men are weak.
A united unit is strong.
A divided unit is weak.

Unity works because it enables you to win every battle you fight.
Still, this is the foolish goal of a weak leader.
Avoid battle and make the enemy's men surrender.
This is the right goal for a superior leader.

PICKING THE RIGHT JOB

Everyone depends on the rules of competition.
A focused organization makes you successful.
An unfocused organization doesn't.
A united team can make you successful.
A divided team doesn't.
A concentrated effort makes you successful.
A divided effort doesn't.
Well-integrated skills make you successful.
Disconnected skills don't.
Clear-cut goals make you successful.
Confused goals don't.

The more focused you are, the easier it will be to overcome difficulties.
But overcoming difficulty doesn't make a great career.
Avoid difficulties and accomplish your goals easily.
This is the right path for a successful career.

The best policy is to attack while the enemy is still planning.
The next best is to disrupt alliances.
The next best is to attack the opposing army.
The worst is to attack the enemy's cities.

This is what happens when you attack a city.
You can attempt it, but you can't finish it.
First you must make siege engines.
You need the right equipment and machinery.
You use three months and still cannot win.
Then, you try to encircle the area.
You use three more months without making progress.
The commander still doesn't win and this angers him.
He then tries to swarm the city.
This kills a third of his officers and men.
He still isn't able to draw the enemy out of the city.
This attack is a disaster.

Make good use of war.
Make the enemy's troops surrender.
You can do this fighting only minor battles.
You can draw their men out of their cities.
You can do it with small attacks.
You can destroy the men of a nation.
You must keep your campaign short.

It's best to find a new role while it is still being planned.
The next best is to get a job through connections.
The next best is to win a position by beating competitors.
The worst is to go after some else's secure position.

What happens when you go after an entrenched position?
You can try for that job, but you won't win it.
First, you must build a case against the current job holder.
You need to find evidence and examples of problems.
This takes months, and they still won't be accepted.
You then try to build a circle of supporters.
After more months of work, you won't make progress.
You will get frustrated and angry.
You then attack the current jobholder directly.
This costs you more credibility.
You are still unable to dislodge him from his position.
This type of job-seeking is disastrous.

Build your career wisely.
Let people give jobs to you.
You can get jobs without fighting for a new position.
You can go around people in entrenched roles.
You get jobs by getting small promotions.
You win away their responsibilities.
You must keep your goals focused.

You must use total war, fighting with everything you have.
Never stop fighting when at war.
You can gain complete advantage.
To do this, you must plan your strategy of attack.

The rules for making war are:
If you outnumber the enemy ten to one, surround them.
If you outnumber them five to one, attack them.
If you outnumber them two to one, divide them.
If you are equal, then find an advantageous battle.
If you are fewer, defend against them.
If you are much weaker, evade them.

Small forces are not powerful.
However, large forces cannot catch them.

You must master command.
The nation must support you.

Supporting the military makes the nation powerful.
Not supporting the military makes the nation weak.

Politicians create problems for the military in three different
ways.
Ignorant of the army's inability to advance, they order an
advance.
Ignorant of the army's inability to withdraw, they order a
withdrawal.
We call this tying up the army.
Politicians don't understand the army's business.
Still, they think they can run an army.
This confuses the army's officers.

Focus totally on your career with everything that you have.
Everything you do matters.
You can gain promote yourself.
To do this, you must plan a strategy for advancement.

Here are the rules for building a career:
If you are already the boss, expand your operation.
If you are near the top, get more aggressive.
If you are further down, invent your own division.
If you are a low-level manager, outperform the others.
If you are an experienced employee, defend your expertise.
If you are a new employee, develop a special skill.

New employees are not critical.
However, large companies cannot do without them.

You must be willing to manage.
Your organization will value you.

Advancing careers makes an organization successful.
Not advancing careers makes an organization weak.

Bad managers create problems for your career in three
different ways.
Ignorant of what your lack of skills, they put you in a
position to fail.
Ignorant of what you can accomplish, they hold you back
from succeeding.
This is hamstringing your efforts.
Poor managers don't understand your skills and goals.
They think they are helping your career.
This only confuses other managers.

Politicians don't know the army's chain of command.
They give the army too much freedom.
This will create distrust among the army's officers.

The entire army becomes confused and distrusting.
This invites invasion from many different rivals.
We say correctly that disorder in an army kills victory.

You must know five things to win:
Victory comes from knowing when to attack and when to
avoid battle.
Victory comes from correctly using large and small forces.
Victory comes from everyone sharing the same goals.
Victory comes from finding opportunities in problems.
Victory comes from having a capable commander and the
government leaving him alone.
You must know these five things.
You then know the theory of victory.

We say:
"Know yourself and know your enemy.
You will be safe in every battle.
You may know yourself but not know the enemy.
You will then lose one battle for every one you win.
You may not know yourself or the enemy.
You will then lose every battle."

Bad managers do not understand how to advance you.
They don't make it clear what you should do.
This creates uncertainty in your career.

When careers are confused, everyone is distrusting.
This invites internal political bickering.
Lack of clear goals destroys your chances of success.

You must know five things to advance your career:
Success comes from knowing when to make a change and
when to stay where you are.
Success comes from performing small and large functions.
Success comes from sharing your organization's goals.
Success comes from turning problems into opportunities.
Success comes from learning to manage and avoiding
internal politics.
You must know these five things.
You then know the philosophy of building a career.

Experience says this:
Know your abilities and your limitations.
If you do, you will be safe making any change.
You may know your abilities but not your limitations.
Then, for every successful position, you will fail in another.
You may know neither your abilities nor your limitations.
Then, you will fail in every position.

27

POSITIONING

Learn from the history of successful battles.
Your first actions should deny victory to the enemy.
You pay attention to your enemy to find the way to win.
You alone can deny victory to the enemy.
Only your enemy can allow you to win.

You must fight well.
You can prevent the enemy's victory.
You cannot win unless the enemy enables your victory.

We say:
You see the opportunity for victory; you don't create it.

You are sometimes unable to win.
You must then defend.
You will eventually be able to win.
You must then attack.
Defend when you have insufficient strength to win.
Attack when you have more strength than you need to win.

Work Experience

Learn from the history of successful people.
First, you must preserve your existing job.
You pay attention to the job market to find advancement.
You alone can preserve your existing position.
Only others create a new position for your advancement.

You must perform well.
You can prevent losing your job.
You cannot win a new job unless others create it for you.

The truth is simple.
You must discover a new position; you do not create it.

You cannot always find a new position.
You must then concentrate on your existing position.
You will eventually discover a better position.
Then you must go after that position.
Stay when you are not qualified to get a better position.
Go after a better position when you a more than qualified.

29

You must defend yourself well.
Save your forces and dig in.
You must attack well.
Move your forces when you have a clear advantage.

You must protect your forces until you can completely
triumph.

Some may see how to win.
However, they cannot position their forces where they must.
This demonstrates limited ability.

Some can struggle to a victory and the whole world may
praise their winning.
This also demonstrates a limited ability.

Win as easily as picking up a fallen hair.
Don't use all of your forces.
See the time to move.
Don't try to find something clever.
Hear the clap of thunder.
Don't try to hear something subtle.

Learn from the history of successful battles.
Victory goes to those who make winning easy.
A good battle is one that you will obviously win.
It doesn't take intelligence to win a reputation.
It doesn't take courage to achieve success.

You must handle your existing responsibilities well.
Develop your experience and dig in.
You must campaign for a new job well.
Go after a new position as soon as you are qualified for it.

Keep getting experience until you are certain you win a
better position.

8—★

You may see a new position that you would like.
Yet you do not see how to qualify yourself for that position.
This shows limited ability.

You may win a better position for which you are poorly
qualified.
This also shows limited ability.

Move to new positions effortless.
Avoid risking your current job.
Watch for the right time to move.
Do not try to be too clever.
Learning about opportunities is easy if you listen.
Don't imagine opportunities where there are none.

Learn from the successful careers of others.
Good jobs go to people who make hiring them easy.
A good position is one that you can obviously win.
It does not take a genius to develop a good reputation.
You do not have to take risks to advance your career.

31

You must win your battles without effort.
Avoid difficult struggles.
Fight when your position must win.
You always win by preventing your defeat.

You must engage only in winning battles.
Position yourself where you cannot lose.
Never waste an opportunity to defeat your enemy.

You win a war by first assuring yourself of victory.
Only afterward do you look for a fight.
Outmaneuver the enemy before the battle and then fight to
win.

You must make good use of war.
Study military philosophy and the art of defense.
You can control your victory or defeat.

This is the art of war.
1. Discuss the distances.
2. Discuss your numbers.
3. Discuss your calculations.
4. Discuss your decisions.
5. Discuss victory.
The ground determines the distance.
The distance determines your numbers.
Your numbers determine your calculations.
Your calculations determine your decisions.
Your decisions determine your victory.

You want to win a new position without effort.
Avoid highly competitive situations.
Go after jobs when your experience will win it.
You get experience by developing your existing job.

You must engage only in successful job moves.
Get the experience that makes you successful.
Never pass by an opportunity to advance your career.

You win better jobs by developing skills and experience.
Only then do you search for a better position.
Expand your current responsibilities before advancing and
then look for a better job.

You must build your career carefully.
Study your profession and improve your performance.
You alone determine your success or failure.

Successful career building requires:
1. a discussion of responsibilities,
2. a discussion of the qualifications,
3. a discussion of the job fit,
4. a discussion of your application,
5. and a discussion of your advancement.
An employer's needs determine the responsibilities.
These responsibilities determine the qualifications.
The qualifications determine the job fit.
The job fit determines the nature of your application.
Your application determines your advancement.

Creating a winning war is like balancing a coin of gold against
a coin of silver.
Creating a losing war is like balancing coin of a silver against
a coin of gold.

Winning a battle is always a matter of people.
You pour them into battle like a flood of water pouring into a
deep gorge.
This is a matter of positioning.

You want positions that offer you more opportunities than your current position offers.
You don't want positions when they offer fewer opportunities than your current position offers.

Winning advancement always depends on qualifications. When you find the right new position, your qualifications should be irresistible.
This depends on your experience.

MOMENTUM

You control a large army as you control a few men.
You just divide their ranks correctly.
You fight a large army the same as you fight a small one.
You only need the right position and communication.
You may meet a large enemy army.
You must be able to encounter the enemy without being
defeated.
You must correctly use both surprise and direct action.
Your army's position must increase your strength.
Troops flanking an enemy can smash them like eggs.
You must correctly use both strength and weakness.

It is the same in all battles.
You use a direct approach to engage the enemy.
You use surprise to win.

You must use surprise for a successful invasion.
Surprise is as infinite as the weather and land.
Surprise is as inexhaustible as the flow of a river.

Career Momentum

You manage large projects as you manage small ones.
You need only to organize your resources correctly.
Solving big problems is the same as solving small ones.
You need the right experience and communication skills.
You may meet difficult challenges.
You can address any difficulty without failing in your
responsibility.
You need to use both creative and standard procedures.
Your experience will increase your ability.
Find a new perspective that eliminates the problem.
You must leverage both your strengths and weaknesses.

It is the same in all jobs.
You must take standard procedures to address problems.
Use creative procedures to solve problems.

You must use creativity to succeed in your career.
There are an infinite number of new ideas.
Creativity utilizes the changes around you.

You can be stopped and yet recover the initiative.
You must use your days and months correctly.

If you are defeated, you can recover.
You must use the four seasons correctly.

There are only a few notes in the scale.
Yet, you can always rearrange them.
You can never hear every song of victory.

There are only a few basic colors.
Yet, you can always mix them.
You can never see all the shades of victory.

There are only a few flavors.
Yet, you can always blend them.
You can never taste all the flavors of victory.

You fight with momentum.
There are only a few types of surprises and direct actions.
Yet, you can always vary the ones you use.
There is no limit to the ways you can win.

Surprise and direct action give birth to each other.
They proceed from each other in an endless cycle.
You can not exhaust all their possible combinations!

Yesterday's failure can become tomorrow's success.
You must make progress every day.

You can make mistakes and still recover.
You must learn to leverage changes over time.

There are only a few basic issues in any problem.
But you can look at these issues any number of ways.
You can always discover a way to address the problem.

There are only a few basic responsibilities in any job.
Yet you can re-prioritize them at any time.
You will never exhaust all the paths to success.

There are only a few measures of productivity.
Yet they can be blended in any number of ways.
You will never run out of improvements you can make.

You build a career with momentum.
You can always use creative and standard procedures.
You can use them to continually change your approach.
There is no limit to succeeding in your position.

Creativity and standard procedures each require the other.
Creativity leads to standards and standards to creativity.
Using both, you will never run out of good ideas.

Surging water flows together rapidly.
Its pressure washes away boulders.
This is momentum.

A hawk suddenly strikes a bird.
Its contact alone kills the prey.
This is timing.

You must fight only winning battles.
Your momentum must be overwhelming.
Your timing must be exact.

Your momentum is like the tension of a bent crossbow.
Your timing is like the pulling of a trigger.

War is complicated and confused.
Battle is chaotic.
Nevertheless, you must not allow chaos.

War is sloppy and messy.
Positions turn around.
Nevertheless, you must never be defeated.

Chaos gives birth to control.
Fear gives birth to courage.
Weakness gives birth to strength.

You must control chaos.
This depends on your planning.
Your men must brave their fears.
This depends on their momentum.

Creative actions fix problems quickly.
Such success creates a strong sense of capability.
This is career momentum.

A successful person identifies a more important role.
Asking alone secures the position.
This is career timing.

You must be successful in your role.
Your career momentum must be noticeable.
Your career timing must be exact.

Success in your current job creates tension.
Asking for a new position releases that tension.

The job market is always complicated and confusing.
Personnel management is always difficult.
You must make hiring and promoting you easy.

Job responsibilities are frequently unclear.
Roles are constantly changing.
Nevertheless, you must always be solving problems.

The job market's confusion requires clear qualifications.
The employer's fear of hiring demands your confidence.
The organization's need requires your abilities.

You must clarify what qualifications are needed.
This depends on your career planning.
Your confidence must overcome employer's fears.
This depends on your career momentum.

You have strengths and weaknesses.
These come from your position.

You must force the enemy to move to your advantage.
Use your position.
The enemy must follow you.
Surrender a position.
The enemy must take it.
You can offer an advantage to move him.
You can use your men to move him.
You use your strength to hold him.

You want a successful battle.
To do this, you must seek momentum.
Do not just demand a good fight from your people.
You must pick good people and then give them momentum.

You must create momentum.
You create it with your men during battle.
This is comparable to rolling trees and stones.
Trees and stones roll because of their shape and weight.
Offer men safety and they will stay calm.
Endanger them and they will act.
Give them a place and they will hold.
Round them up and they will march.

You make your men powerful in battle with momentum.
This is just like rolling round stones down over a high, steep
cliff.
Use your momentum.

You have both strengths and weaknesses.
They arise from your experience.

You want employers to give you the positions you desire.
Use your experience.
Employers must want you.
Give up something.
Employers must meet you halfway.
You can offer a concession to help them hire you.
You can use your success to seek advancement.
You use your skills to keep your employer happy.

You want a successful career.
You need career momentum.
Do not just simply demand recognition for your abilities.
Find a good employer and generate career momentum.

You must create momentum in your career.
You do this by doing more than your job requires.
Your responsibilities should flow together.
They should create an important and meaningful position.
Give employers confidence and they will stay with you.
Give them the fear they might lose you and they will act.
Have them give you a position that will keep you.
Clarify your responsibilities so you can act.

You make abilities meaningful with career momentum.
Portray your career as success naturally following upon
success.
Use your momentum.

WEAKNESS AND STRENGTH

Always arrive first to the empty battlefield to await the
enemy at your leisure.
If you are late and hurry to the battlefield, fighting is more
difficult.

You want a successful battle.
Move your men, but not into opposing forces.

You can make the enemy come to you.
Offer him an advantage.
You can make the enemy avoid coming to you.
Threaten him with danger.

When the enemy is fresh, you can tire him.
When he is well fed, you can starve him.
When he is relaxed, you can move him.

44

ORGANIZATIONAL POLITICS

You want the advantage of getting to a good company
before others do.
Avoid moving to companies where rivals are entrenched in
the best jobs.

You want a successful career.
Change positions, but don't go where you have rivals.

You can make employers come to you.
Let them know you are interested.
You can avoid the jobs that you don't want.
Make it seem expensive to hire you.

If employers feel well-staffed, make them feel a lack.
If employers feel satisfied, make them hungry for more.
If employers feel comfortable, make them restless.

Leave any place without haste.
Hurry to where you are not expected.
You can easily march hundreds of miles without tiring.
To do so, travel through areas that are deserted.
You must take whatever you attack.
Attack when there is no defense.
You must have walls to defend.
Defend where it is impossible to attack.

Be skilled in attacking.
Give the enemy no idea of where to defend.

Be skillful in your defense.
Give the enemy no idea of where to attack.

Be subtle! Be subtle!
Arrive without any clear formation.
Quietly! Quietly!
Arrive without a sound.
You must use all your skill to control the enemy's decisions.

Advance to where they can't defend.
Charge through their openings.
Withdraw where the enemy cannot chase you.
Move quickly so that they cannot catch you.

Never leave an existing job in a hurry.
Move to new jobs when it is least expected.
You can change to a completely different type of industry.
But that industry must be hungry for new people.
You must get the positions you go after.
Go after employers that need your skills.
The jobs that you win must be easy to hold.
Get hired where it will be difficult to lose your job.

Be skilled in winning jobs.
Know what an employer's needs are.

Be skilled in keeping jobs.
Give employers no idea of what your weaknesses are.

Keep your own counsel.
Don't go into a new job with a clear agenda.
You must be careful.
Don't make waves in a new position.
You must skillfully control employers' perceptions.

Look to get promoted where your employer needs help.
Aggressively fill the job opening.
Make sure that problems don't catch up to you.
Move up the organization's ranks quickly.

I always pick my own battles.
The enemy can hide behind high walls and deep trenches.
I do not try to win by fighting him directly.
Instead, I attack a place that he must rescue.
I avoid the battles that I don't want.
I can divide the ground and yet defend it.
I don't give the enemy anything to win.
Divert him from coming to where you defend.

I make their men take a position while I take none.
I then focus my forces where the enemy divides his forces.
Where I focus, I unite my forces.
When the enemy divides, he creates many small groups.
I want my large group to attack one of his small ones.
Then I have many men where the enemy has but a few.
My large force can overwhelm his small one.
I then go on to the next small enemy group.
I will take them one at a time.

We must keep the place that we've chosen as a battleground
a secret.
The enemy must not know.
Force the enemy to prepare his defense in many places.
I want the enemy to defend many places.
Then I can choose where to fight.
His forces will be weak there.

You must pick your internal battles.
Rivals can be well ensconced in entrenched positions.
You can't overcome them by direct confrontation.
Instead, question performance that they have to defend.
Avoid confrontations you don't want.
Divide responsibilities so that you can defend your area.
Don't leave rivals anything to win by attacking you.
Distract rivals from getting involved in your affairs.

Make others express their ideas before you voice yours.
Concentrate your thinking on the gaps in their plans.
When you take a position, bring people together.
Let rivals divide the organization into small groups.
Unite a large group against the interests of a few.
You want the interest of the organization on your side.
You can easily beat a rival's small group.
You can then go onto the next rival's group.
Tackle them one at a time.

You must keep your plans to oppose specific projects a secret.
Your rivals must never know.
Encourage them to defend all of their positions.
They must spread themselves too thin.
You can then choose the project to attack.
They will be weak there.

If he reinforces his front lines, he depletes his rear.
If he reinforces his rear, he depletes his front.
If he reinforces his right, he depletes his left.
If he reinforces his left, he depletes his right.
Without knowing the place of attack, he cannot prepare.
Without a place, he will be weak everywhere.

The enemy has weak points.
Prepare your men against them.
He has strong points.
Make his men prepare themselves against you.

You must know the battle ground.
You must know the time of battle.
You can then travel a thousand miles and still win the battle.

The enemy should not know the battleground.
He shouldn't know the time of battle.
His left will be unable to support his right.
His right will be unable to support his left.
His front lines will be unable to support his rear.
His rear will be unable to support his front.
His support is distant even if it is only ten miles away.
What unknown place can be close?

We control the balance of forces.
The enemy may have many men but they are superfluous.
How can they help him to victory?

People get support for one pet project at the cost of another.
They increase the budget in one area by decreasing another.
They add people to one group by taking them from another.
They spend more time in one place by neglecting others.
No one has enough resources to do everything.
This creates weak points that can be identified.

Your rivals have weak points.
Prepare yourself to address them.
Rivals have strong points.
They will abandon them if they are worried about you.

You must know where your organization needs help.
You must know when acting will help it.
Even if the project is difficult, you can make it successful.

Your rivals must not know what projects you plan.
They must never know when your projects start.
Rivals cannot then line up opposition to these projects.
Rivals cannot then draw away funding from those projects.
Rivals cannot keep people from joining these projects.
They cannot distract you from focusing on those projects.
Rivals must be ignorant even of projects that affect them.
If they don't know your plans, how can they fight you?

You decide the balance of power when you pick a project.
Rivals may be powerful, but their ignorance disarms them.
How can their influence hurt you?

We say:
You must let victory happen.

The enemy may have many men.
You can still control him without a fight.

When you form your strategy, know the strengths and
weaknesses of your plan.
When you execute, know how to manage both action and
inaction.
When you take a position, know the deadly and the winning
grounds.
When you battle, know when you have too many or too few
men.

Use your position as your war's centerpiece.
Arrive at the battle without a formation.
Don't take a position.
Then even the best spies can't report it.
Even the wisest general cannot plan to counter you.
Take a position where you can triumph using superior
numbers.
Keep the enemy's forces ignorant.
Their troops will learn of my location when my position will
win.
They must not know how our location gives us a winning
position.
Make the battle one from which they cannot recover.
You must always adjust your position to their position.

The truth is plain.
You must let yourself be successful.

Your opponents can be numerous.
You can still control them while avoiding a confrontation.

8━┳

When you shape a career plan, know the strengths and
weaknesses of your organization.
When you plan a project, know what needs to be done and
what doesn't.
When you take a position, know what position will win and
what will lose.
When you face rivals, know when you have support and
when you do not.

Use your experience as your career's centerpiece.
Go into an organization without an agenda.
Avoid getting categorized.
Then even your opponents can't speak against you.
Even the most senior manager cannot oppose you.
Plan projects that have broad support within the
organization.
Keep your rivals in the dark.
Rivals should only learn about your projects when the
projects are successful.
They should not know how you made your project a
success.
Make sure that rivals cannot steal the credit from you.
When they change their positions, adjust your plans.

8━┳

Manage your military position like water.
Water takes every shape.
It avoids the high and moves to the low.
Your war can take any shape.
It must avoid the strong and strike the weak.
Water follows the shape of the land that directs its flow.
Your forces follow the enemy who determines how you win.

Make war without a standard approach.
Water has no consistent shape.
If you follow the enemy's shifts and changes, you can always win.
We call this shadowing.

Fight five different campaigns without a firm rule for victory.
Use all four seasons without a consistent position.
Your timing must be sudden.
A few weeks determine your failure or success.

You must remain flexible in your organization.
You must do whatever needs to be done.
Avoid creating high expectations.
You can adjust to any situation.
Look for problems you can turn into successes.
Let the needs of the organization dictate your actions.
Your success comes from addressing those needs.

You must avoid rigid ideas about your career path.
A successful career can take any shape.
If you follow shifts and changes in your organization you can always win.
This is called shadowing.

In each new job, be open to a new approach.
Use the current trends to form your opinions.
You must act quickly.
The initial impression you make determines your success.

ARMED CONFLICT

Everyone uses the arts of war.
You accept orders from the government.
Then you assemble your army.
You organize your men and build camps.
You must avoid disasters from armed conflict.

Seeking armed conflict can be disastrous.
Because of this, a detour can be the shortest path.
Because of this, problems can become opportunities.

Use an indirect route as your highway.
Use the search for advantage to guide you.
When you fall behind, you must catch up.
When you get ahead, you must wait.
You must know the detour that most directly accomplishes
your plan.

Undertake armed conflict when you have an advantage.
Seeking armed conflict for its own sake is dangerous.

Internal Conflict

Everyone wants to build their career.
You get goals from your superiors.
Then you assemble your resources.
You organize your tasks and prioritize.
You must then avoid problems from internal conflict.

Internal conflict is costly to your career.
Because of this, you must be willing to compromise.
You must turn potential conflicts into opportunities.

You must go out of your way to avoid conflict.
Let your search for success guide you.
If you fall behind in your job, you must catch up.
If you get too far ahead of schedule, you must wait.
You must find a way of fulfilling your mission without hurting others.

Seek to best others only when it will help your career.
It is foolish to get involved in conflict accidentally.

You can build up an army to fight for an advantage.
Then you won't catch the enemy.
You can force your army to go fight for an advantage.
Then you abandon your heavy supply wagons.

You keep only your armor and hurry straight after the enemy.
You avoid stopping day or night.
You use many roads at the same time.
You go hundreds of miles to fight for an advantage.
Then the enemy catches your commanders and your army.
Your strong soldiers get there first.
Your weaker soldiers follow behind.
Using this approach, only one in ten will arrive.
You can try to go fifty miles to fight for an advantage.
Then your commanders and army will stumble.
Using this method, only half of your soldiers will make it.
You can try to go thirty miles to fight for an advantage.
Then only two out of three get there.

If you make your army travel without good supply lines, they
will die.
Without supplies and food, your army will die.
If you don't save the harvest, your army will die.

You think you can build up support to win a conflict.
Then your rival will make you look foolish.
You can get caught up with the idea of beating a rival.
You then forget you are part of an organization.

You can try to protect yourself and prove a rival wrong.
You can work day and night.
You can try to cover all your bases.
You can make real progress trying to show up an opponent.
Then your rival finds a problem with you or your project.
Your progress is forgotten.
Your problems are what people see.
Only a small fraction of your efforts will be rewarded.
You can try changing your plan to oppose a rival.
You will then make a foolish mistake.
You will be only half as successful as you could be.
You may go a little out of your way to attack a rival.
It will cost you more than it is worth.

If you try to build a career without getting broad support,
you will fail.
Without focusing your time and efforts, you will fail.
If you do not concentrate on your mission, you will fail.

Do not let any of your potential enemies know of what you
are planning.
You must stay with the enemy.
You must know the lay of the land.
You must know where the obstructions are.
You must know where the marshes are.
If you don't, you cannot move the army.
You must use local guides.
If you don't, you can't take advantage of the terrain.

You make war using a deceptive position.
If you use deception, then you can move.
Using deception, you can upset the enemy and change the
situation.
You must move as quickly as the wind.
You must rise like the forest.
You must invade and plunder like fire.
You must stay as motionless as a mountain.
You must be as mysterious as the fog.
You must strike like sounding thunder.

Divide your troops to plunder the villages.
When on open ground, dividing is an advantage.
Don't worry about organization, just move.
Be the first to find a new route that leads directly to a winning
plan.
This is the how you are successful at armed conflict.

Instead, you must keep quiet about what project you are planning.
You must stay close to your rivals.
You must know your business.
You must know where the potential problems are.
You must know where you might get bogged down.
If you don't, you can't move ahead.
You must develop information sources.
If you don't, you won't get ahead in the organization.

You must disguise your intentions to overcome rivals.
Controlling people's perceptions, you can succeed.
Controlling people's perceptions, you can outpace rivals and win promotions.
You must work quickly and stay focused.
Get noticed by superiors but overlooked by rivals.
You must generate value for your organization.
You must not attract unwanted attention.
You must keep quiet about your career plans.
You must stand out from the crowd.

Use half your efforts to make your progress clear.
When making good progress, take some time to advertise it.
Don't worry about others; just keep going.
Be the first to make a breakthrough success for your organization.
This is the how you are successful at internal contests.

Military experience says:
"You can speak, but you will not be heard.
You must use gongs and drums.
You cannot really see your forces just by looking.
You must use banners and flags."

You must master gongs, drums, banners and flags.
Place people as a single unit where they can all see and hear.
You must unite them as one.
Then, the brave cannot advance alone.
The fearful cannot withdraw alone.
You must force them to act as a group.

In night battles, you must use numerous fires and drums.
In day battles, you must use many banners and flags.
You must position your people to control what they see and
hear.

You control your army by controlling its emotions.
As a general, you must be able to control emotions.

In the morning, a person's energy is high.
During the day, it fades.
By evening, a person's thoughts turn to home.
You must use your troops wisely.
Avoid the enemy's high spirits.
Strike when they are lazy and want to go home.
This is how you master energy.

Career experience teaches us this:
"You can be successful, but it will be overlooked.
You must promote your success to get noticed.
Superiors cannot know your capabilities just by looking.
You must make your success into news."

Use reports and gimmicks to get your superiors' attention.
Make sure that your successes are widely known.
Use success to bring the organization together.
Do not try to take credit alone.
Give credit to everyone involved.
You want to be seen as acting for the best of the group.

When you are unknown and remote, you advertise more.
If you are better known, you must still promote yourself.
You must consider what people at every level of the
company see and hear.

You control your career by considering people's feelings.
You must also control your emotions.

In the morning, people are busy.
During the day, their energy fades.
In the evening, people want to go home.
You must time your efforts wisely.
Avoid bothering people when they are busy.
Get their agreement when they want to go home.
This is how you make agreement easy.

Use discipline to await the chaos of battle.
Keep relaxed to await a crisis.
This is how you master emotion.

Stay close to home to await a distant enemy.
Stay comfortable to await the weary enemy.
Stay well fed to await the hungry enemy.
This is how you master power.

Don't entice the enemy when their ranks are orderly.
You must not attack when their formations are solid
This is how you master adaptation.
You must follow these military rules.
Do not take a position facing the high ground.
Do not oppose those with their backs to wall.
Do not follow those who pretend to flee.
Do not attack the enemy's strongest men.
Do not swallow the enemy's bait.
Do not block an army that is heading home.
Leave an escape outlet for a surrounded army.
Do not press a desperate foe.
This is the art of war.

When internal problems arise, don't overreact.
Keep calm in every crisis.
This is how you master your own emotions.

Stay close to your duties, and critics will be frustrated.
Stay well prepared, and critics will be unprepared.
Stay within budget, and critics will have no ammunition.
This is how you master power.

Do not tempt rivals when they are well prepared.
You must avoid conflict when rivals are well connected.
This is how you master adapting.
You must follow these rules in your career:
Do not offer an opinion that contradicts your superiors.
Do not criticize without offering alternatives.
Do not follow those who have failed in the past.
Do not attack your rival's successes.
Do not believe everything you hear.
Do not create problems for others.
Leave every critic a way to save face.
Do not create unhappy coworkers.
This is the art of building a career.

ADAPTABILITY

Everyone uses the arts of war.
As a general, you get your orders from the government.
You gather your troops.
On dangerous ground, you must not camp.
Where the roads intersect, you must join your allies.
When an area is cut off, you must not delay in it.
When you are surrounded, you must scheme.
In a life-or-death situation, you must fight.
There are roads that you must not take.
There are armies that you must not fight.
There are strongholds that you must not attack.
There are positions that you must not defend.
There are government commands that must not be obeyed.

Military leaders must be experts in knowing how to adapt to
win.
This will teach you the use of war.

FLEXIBILITY IN YOUR CAREER

These are basic rules of building a career.
You get direction from your superiors.
Then you organize your resources.
In difficult environments, you must not get comfortable
Where interests intersect, you must find allies.
If a job is a dead-end, you must avoid it.
If you feel hemmed in, you must get creative.
When you are in a do-or-die situation, you must perform.
There are career paths that you must avoid.
There are political battles that you must not fight.
There are entrenched positions that you cannot win.
There are positions in which you cannot succeed.
There are boss's instructions that you must ignore.

You must become an expert at knowing how to adapt to
advance your career.
Adaptation is the key to success.

Some commanders are not good at making adjustments to
find an advantage.
They can know the shape of the terrain.
Still, they can not find an advantageous position.

Some military commanders do not know how to adjust their
methods.
They can find an advantageous position.
Still, they can not use their men effectively.

You must be creative in your planning.
You must adapt to your opportunities and weaknesses.
You can use a variety of approaches and still have a
consistent result.
You must adjust to a variety of problems and consistently
solve them.

You can deter your potential enemy by using his weaknesses
against him.
You can keep your enemy's army occupied by giving it work
to do.
You can rush your enemy by offering him an advantageous
position.

Some people are unable to adapt their viewpoint to finding a new opportunity.
They can understand the changing job market.
Still, they cannot see their opportunity in it.

Some people are unable to adapt their experience to fit a desired job.
They can see a good opportunity in the market.
Still, they cannot qualify themselves for it.

You must get inventive in advancing your career.
You must adapt to your opportunities and difficulties.
You can use different approaches and still consistently move your career forward.
You can face a variety of problems and consistently find a way to solve them.

You can win any position by using the employer's needs against him.
You must interest an employer by giving him a problem to think about.
You can hasten the decision by offering the employer a reason to decide now.

You must make use of war.
Do not trust that the enemy isn't coming.
Trust your readiness to meet him.
Do not trust that the enemy won't attack.
We must rely only on our ability to pick a place that the
enemy can't attack.

You can exploit five different faults in a leader.
If he is willing to die, you can kill him.
If he wants to survive, you can capture him.
He may have a quick temper.
You can then provoke him with insults.
If he has a delicate sense of honor, you can disgrace him.
If he loves his people, you can create problems for him.
In every situation, look for these five weaknesses.
They are common faults in commanders.
They always lead to military disaster.

To overturn an army, you must kill its general.
To do this, you must use these five weaknesses.
You must always look for them.

You must always be working on your career.
Do not think that you don't have an opportunity to advance.
Instead, be ready to meet the opportunity should it arise.
Do not trust that your current position is safe.
Instead, work to make yourself indispensable in your current position.

You can use five different weaknesses in a superior.
If a superior is willing to be replaced, you can replace him.
If he wants to stay where he is, you can get his support.
Some superiors overreact.
You can manipulate their emotions.
If a superior is honorable, you make him indebted to you.
If he cares for his people, you can become his protégé.
In every situation, look for these five characteristics.
Look for these characteristics in your managers.
They can help you avoid career disaster.

Advancing in some organizations means replacing the boss.
You must know how to exploit his weaknesses.
You must always be aware of them.

ARMED MARCH

Everyone moving their army must adjust to the enemy.

Keep out of the mountains and in the valleys.
Position yourself on the heights facing the sun.
To win your battles, never attack uphill.
This is how you position your army in the mountains.

When water blocks you, keep far away from it.
Let the enemy cross the river and wait for him.
Do not meet him in midstream.
Wait for him to get half his forces across and then take
advantage of the situation.

You need to be able to fight.
You can't do that if you are in the water when you meet an
attack.
Position yourself upstream, facing the sun.
Never face against the current.
Always position your army upstream when near the water.

Your Career Path

In any career path, you adjust to the situation.

Keep out of large organizations and stick to smaller ones.
If in a large organization, look for high, more visible roles.
To be successful, respect the organization's hierarchy.
This is how to manage a career in a large organization.

If reorganization blocks you, distance yourself from it.
Let others get involved with reorganization.
Do not attack rivals during this type of change.
Wait to see what happens to see if you can take advantage
of the situation.

You need to perform successfully.
You can't be successful if you are caught up in
reorganization.
Position yourself visibly in an organization's future.
Never fight against organizational trends.
Position yourself with the trends during reorganization.

You may have to move across marshes.
Move through them quickly without stopping.
You may meet the enemy in the middle of a marsh.
You must keep on the water grasses.
Keep your back to a clump of trees.
This is how you position your army in a marsh.

On a level plateau, take a position that you can change.
Keep the higher ground on your right and to the rear.
Keep the danger in front of you and safety behind.
This is how you position yourself on a level plateau.

You can find an advantage in all four of these situations.
Learn from the great emperor who used positioning to
conquer his four rivals.

Armies are stronger on high ground and weaker on low.
They are better camping on sunny, southern hillsides than on
the shady, northern ones.
Provide for your army's health and place it well.
Your army will be free from disease.
Done correctly, this means victory.

You must sometimes defend on a hill or riverbank.
You must keep on the south side in the sun.
Keep the uphill slope at your right rear.

This will give the advantage to your army.
It will always give you a position of strength.

Your career path may take you into temporary jobs.
Get out of these positions as quickly as you can.
You may meet difficulty in a temporary position.
Ally yourself with the stable parts of the organization.
Defend your role and your value.
This is how you manage your career in a temporary job.

In flat organizations, keep yourself flexible.
Keep yourself visible and keep the management with you.
Face your challenges and defend your actions.
This is how you manage a career in a flat organization.

You can find opportunities in any situation.
Learn from the success of the winners who discover
opportunities in every situation.

Careers are stronger with skills and weaker without them.
You are better off in a visible, active role than in a quiet,
hidden one.
Keep your career healthy, accepting only good positions.
Your worth to the organization will be free from criticism.
Do this correctly and you will be successful.

Sometimes you must defend a project or a change.
Highlight the project's value to everyone.
Keep upper management behind you.

This will create opportunities in your career path.
This will always give you a position of strength.

Stop the march when the rain swells the river into rapids.
You may want to ford the river.
Wait until it subsides.

All regions have dead-ends such as waterfalls.
There are deep lakes.
There are high cliffs.
There are dense jungles.
There are thick quagmires.
There are steep crevasses.
Get away from all these quickly.
Do not get close to them.
Keep them at a distance.
Maneuver the enemy close to them.
Position yourself facing these dangers.
Push the enemy back into them.

Danger can hide on your army's flank.
There are reservoirs and lakes.
There are reeds and thickets.
There are forests of trees.
Their dense vegetation provides a hiding place.
You must cautiously search through them.
They can always hide an ambush.

Stop seeking advancement during shift in your industry.
You want to survive a transition.
Wait until the changes subside.

All organizations have dead ends.
There are positions too difficult to perform.
There are positions that are too highly paid.
There are positions that no one sees.
There are positions that are doomed to fail.
There are jobs that offer no advancement.
Keep away from these positions.
Never accept them.
Don't let them become your problem.
Let your rivals struggle with them.
Identify these positions in the organization.
Suggest others for them.

Your career can be blind sided.
Beware of organizational habits and prejudices.
Beware of making false assumptions.
Beware of well established people.
The entrenched can be the basis for unpleasant surprises.
You must take time to learn about the organization.
Don't be taken unawares.

Sometimes, the enemy is close by but remains calm.
Expect to find him in a natural stronghold.
Other times, he remains at a distance but provokes battle.
He wants you to attack him.

He sometimes shifts the position of his camp.
He is looking for an advantageous position.

The trees in the forest move.
Expect that the enemy is coming.
The tall grasses obstruct your view.
Be suspicious.

The birds take flight.
Expect that the enemy is hiding.
Animals startle.
Expect an ambush.

Notice the dust.
It sometimes rises high in a straight line.
Vehicles are coming.
The dust appears low in a wide band.
Foot soldiers are coming.
The dust seems scattered in different areas.
The enemy is collecting firewood.
Any dust is light and settling down.
The enemy is setting up camp.

A potential employer seems interested but is quiet.
You should expect that he is well staffed.
Another possible employer seems distant but keeps contact.
He wants you to sell yourself to him.

A potential employer changes the position he offers.
He sees hiring you as an opportunity.

You hear of changes in the job market.
Expect that an employer is active.
People are keeping secrets from you.
Be suspicious.

Your calls are not answered.
Suspect that an employer is delaying.
Contacts are nervous.
A rival is undercutting you.

Pay attention to rumors.
A rumor can come straight from top management.
Expect a quick job offer.
A rumor seems to be common knowledge.
Expect communication from an employer.
The rumor seems to be scattered here and there.
The employer is thinking of waiting.
Rumors become rarer and rarer.
The employer is waiting.

Your enemy speaks humbly while building up forces.
He is planning to advance.

The enemy talks aggressively and pushes as if to advance.
He is planning to retreat.

Small vehicles exit his camp first and move to positions on
the army's flanks.
They are forming a battle line.

Your enemy tries to sue for peace but without offering a
treaty.
He is plotting.

Your enemy's men run to leave and yet form ranks.
You should expect action.

Half his army advances and the other half retreats.
He is luring you.

Your enemy plans to fight but his men just stand there.
They are starving.

Those who draw water drink it first.
They are thirsty.

Your enemy sees an advantage but does not advance.
His men are tired.

Birds gather.
Your enemy has abandoned his camp.

A potential employer humbly and improves his offer.
He is planning to win you.

A potential employer aggressively demands a decision.
He is going to withdraw his offer.

A potential employer gets tired of waiting and puts a
deadline on your decision.
He has had enough.

A potential employer asks you to stay but doesn't make a
concrete offer.
He is plotting.

A potential employer claims disinterest but counter an offer.
Expect him to come back again.

A potential employer gives into half of your demands.
He is tempting you.

A potential employer plans to hire you but makes no offer.
He is out of resources.

An employer is concerned about when to pay you.
He is short of money.

A potential employer is busy despite his lack of growth.
His people are overworked.

The phone isn't answered.
A potential employer has gone out of business.

Your enemy's soldiers call in the night.
They are afraid.

Your enemy's army is raucous.
They do not take their commander seriously.

Your enemy's banners and flags shift.
Order is breaking down.

Your enemy's officers are irritable.
They are exhausted.

Your enemy's men kill their horses for meat.
They are out of provisions.

They don't put their pots away or return to their tents.
They expect to fight to the death.

Enemy troops appear sincere and agreeable.
But their men are slow to speak to each other.
They are no longer united.

Your enemy offers too many incentives to his men.
He is in trouble.

Your enemy gives out too many punishments.
His men are weary.

Your enemy first attacks and then is afraid of your larger
force.
His best troops have not arrived.

A potential employer's people secretly complain.
They are unhappy.

A potential employer's people are undisciplined.
They don't take their organization's management seriously.

A potential employer is going through reorganization.
The organization is breaking down.

A potential employer's managers are irritable.
They are stretched thin.

A potential employer is selling off part of his business.
He is short of funds.

A potential employer's key people are leaving.
They expect the organization to fail.

A potential employer's people are polite with one another.
However, they communicate poorly.
They lack a common goal.

A potential employer offers too much compensation.
His organization is in trouble.

A potential employer is strict about meeting quotas.
He is under pressure.

A potential employer first actively courts you but then
seems afraid to hire you.
He needs approval.

Your enemy comes in a conciliatory manner.
He needs to rest and recuperate.

Your enemy is angry and appears to welcome battle.
This goes on for a long time, but he doesn't attack.
He also doesn't leave the field.
You must watch him carefully.

If you are too weak to fight, you must find more men.
In this situation, you must not act aggressively.
You must unite your forces, expect the enemy, recruit men
and wait.

You must be cautious about making plans and adjust to the
enemy.
You must increase the size of your forces.

With new, undedicated soldiers, you can depend on them if
you discipline them.
They will tend to disobey your orders.
If they do not obey your orders, they will be useless.

You can depend on seasoned, dedicated soldiers.
But you must avoid disciplining them without reason.
Otherwise, you cannot use them.

You must control your soldiers with *esprit de corp*.
You must bring them together by winning victories.
You must get them to believe in you.

A potential employer comes offering more responsibility.
He needs your help.

A potential employer is emotional and appears to want you.
The interview process goes on without an offer.
He remains in contact.
You must maintain your interest.

8—★

If you lack qualifications, you need more experience.
In this situation, don't seek promotion aggressively.
You must focus your efforts, prepare for employment, get
experience, and take your time.

You must move carefully and do whatever your employer
requires.
You must gain more experience.

8—★

You can expand your responsibility with new, untested
skills if you are disciplined.
If you are not disciplined, you will make mistakes.
If you make mistakes, your experience will be of no value.

It is different with established, proven skills.
When you are skilled, you know when you can experiment.
Experience allows you to try new ideas.

You are offered experience when you are enthusiastic.
You must win people over to be successful.
You must get them to believe in you.

Make it easy for them to obey your orders by training your
people.
Your people will then obey you.
If you do not make it easy to obey, you won't train your
people.
Then they will not obey.

Make your commands easy to follow.
You must understand the way a crowd thinks.

Make it easy for people to believe in you by
communicating well.
They will then trust you.
If you do not communicate well, people will not know how
to react to you.
They will not trust you.

Make yourself easy to understand.
You must also understand how other people think.

Field Position

Some field positions are unobstructed.
Some field positions are entangling.
Some field positions are supporting.
Some field positions are constricted.
Some field positions give you a barricade.
Some field positions are spread out.

You can attack from some positions easily.
Others can attack you easily as well.
We call these unobstructed positions.
These positions are open.
On them, be the first to occupy a high, sunny area.
Put yourself where you can defend your supply routes.
Then you will have an advantage.

EVALUATING POSITIONS

Some jobs are without barriers.
Some jobs are risky.
Some jobs are entrenched.
Some jobs are exclusive.
Some jobs are easy to protect.
Some jobs are spread too thin.

You can move up from some jobs easily.
Rivals can move up from these positions easily as well.
These are unobstructed positions.
These jobs offer no barriers to advancement.
In these jobs, seek visibility.
Put yourself in a position where you can protect your back.
Then these jobs offer an opportunity.

You can attack from some positions easily.
Disaster arises when you try to return to them.
These are entangling positions.
These field positions are one-sided.
Wait until your enemy is unprepared.
You can then attack from these positions and win.
Avoid a well prepared enemy.
You will try to attack and lose.
Since you can't return, you will meet disaster.
These field positions offer no advantage.

I cannot leave some positions without losing an advantage.
If the enemy leaves this ground, he also loses an advantage.
We call these supporting field positions.
These positions strengthen you.
The enemy may try to entice me away.
Still, I will hold my position.
You must entice the enemy to leave.
You then strike him as he is leaving.
These field positions offer an advantage.

Some field positions are constricted.
I try to get to these positions before the enemy does.
You must fill these areas and await the enemy.
Sometimes, the enemy will reach them first.
If he fills them, do not follow him.
But if he fails to fill them, you can go after him.

You can move up from some jobs easily.
You cannot get back into these positions after leaving them.
These are risky jobs.
They give you one chance.
Wait until you are prepared to move up.
You can then move from risky positions into new ones.
Avoid moving from these jobs if you aren't ready.
You can win a promotion but then fail in the new position.
If you can't go back to your old job, you are unemployed
These jobs offer no real opportunity.

You cannot leave some jobs without losing an opportunity.
Anyone in this position is going to do well in the future.
This is a job in which you are entrenched.
Know when you are entrenched in your job.
A rival may try to lure you away.
You must hold your position.
If a rival is entrenched, try to lure him away.
You can then go after his job.
Entrenched jobs offer a long-term opportunity.

Some jobs are exclusive.
You must get into these positions before rivals do.
You must perform in these jobs well and keep them.
A rival may get into one of these positions first.
If he performs well, don't try to follow him.
If he fails to perform, you can try to displace him.

Some field positions give you a barricade.
I get to these positions before the enemy does.
You occupy their southern, sunny heights and wait for the
enemy.
Sometimes the enemy occupies these areas first.
If so, entice him away.
Never go after him.

Some field positions are too spread out.
Your force may seem equal to the enemy.
Still you will lose if you provoke a battle.
If you fight, you will not have any advantage.

These are the six types of field positions.
Each battleground has its own rules.
As a commander, you must know where to go.
You must examine each position closely.

Some armies can be outmaneuvered.
Some armies are too lax.
Some armies fall down.
Some armies fall apart.
Some armies are disorganized.
Some armies must retreat.

Know all six of these weaknesses.
They lead to losses on both good and bad ground.
They all arise from the army's commander.

Some jobs are easy to protect.
You must win these positions before rivals do.
You then must make yourself visible and await rivals to criticize you.
Sometimes rivals win these jobs first.
If so, they can only be tempted away.
Never criticize people in these positions.

Some jobs are spread too thin.
They may seem to have power.
Nevertheless, you will never be successful in them.
These jobs offer no real opportunity.

Thus, there are the six types of jobs.
Each type of job has its own rules.
To build a career, you must know which jobs to accept.
You must analyze each position carefully.

8━━🕇

Some organizations are inflexible.
Some organizations are too lax.
Some organizations stumble.
Some organizations self-destruct.
Some organizations are chaotic.
Some organizations are shrinking.

You must recognize these six weaknesses.
These organizational problems affect your success.
These weaknesses come from the organization's leader.

One general can command a force equal to the enemy.
Still his enemy outflanks him.
This means that his army can be outmaneuvered.

Another can have strong soldiers, but weak officers.
This means that his army will be too lax.

Another has strong officers but weak soldiers.
This means that his army will fall down.

Another has sub-commanders that are angry and defiant.
They attack the enemy and fight their own battles.
As a commander, he cannot know the battlefield.
This means that his army will fall apart.

Another general is weak and easygoing.
He fails to make his orders clear.
His officers and men lack direction.
This shows in his military formations.
This means that his army will be disorganized.

Another general fails to predict the enemy.
He pits his small forces against larger ones.
He puts his weak forces against stronger ones.
He fails to pick his fights correctly.
This means that his army must retreat.

You must know all about these six weaknesses.
You must understand the philosophies that lead to defeat.
When a general arrives, you can know what he will do.
You must study each one carefully.

Organizations can look competitive on the outside.
Still, competitors lead the industry.
This means that these organizations are inflexible.

Organizations can have good managers but poor workers.
These organizations are too lax.

Organizations can have good workers but poor managers.
These organizations will stumble.

The organization's managers have their own priorities.
They want to fight each other over resources.
The organization's leader does not understand the politics.
This means that the organization will self-destruct.

Some organizations' leaders are lazy and sloppy.
They fail to make the goals clear.
Their managers and workers both lack direction.
This shows in their lack of organization.
These organizations are chaotic.

Some organizations' leaders fail to predict the future.
They don't see the major trends in the industry.
They are overmatched by their competitors.
They make poor decisions.
These organizations will shrink.

Recognize these six weaknesses in any organization.
You must understand the thinking that leads to failure.
If you take a job in them, you know what will happen.
You must weigh each potential employer carefully.

Y ou must control your field position.
It will always strengthen your army.

You must predict the enemy to overpower him and win.
You must analyze the obstacles, dangers, and distances.
This is the best way to command.

Understand your field position before you go to battle.
Then you will win.
You can fail to understand your field position and still fight.
Then you will lose.

You must provoke battle when you will certainly win.
It doesn't matter what you are ordered.
The government may order you not to fight.
Despite that, you must always fight when you will win.

Sometimes provoking a battle will lead to a loss.
The government may order you to fight.
Despite that, you must avoid battle when you will lose.

You must advance without desiring praise.
You must retreat without fearing shame.
The only correct move is to preserve your troops.
This is how you serve your country.
This is how you reward your nation.

You must control your job situation.
Your control creates success in your career.

You must foresee how to pick the right employer.
You must analyze difficulties, problems, and needs.
This is the best way to build a career.

You must understand these issues when you look for a job.
If you do, you will succeed.
If you fail to find the right position, you can still get a job.
However, you will not be successful.

You must go after a job that will make you successful.
Forget your other priorities.
You may find it difficult to go after this job.
Still, you must go after it when the opportunity is real.

Sometimes, winning a promotion will hurt your career.
Your employer may give you the promotion.
Still, if you accept it, you will fail.

You must never take a job for the sake of pride.
Abandon a "good job" without embarrassment.
Your only goal is to advance your career.
This is how you serve your family.
This is how you ensure your success.

Think of your soldiers as little children.
You can make them follow you into a deep river.
Treat them as your beloved children.
You can lead them all to their deaths.

Some leaders are generous, but cannot use their men.
They love their men, but cannot command them.
Their men are unruly and disorganized.
These leaders create spoiled children.
Their soldiers are useless.

You may know what your soldiers will do in an attack.
You may not know if the enemy is vulnerable to attack.
You will then win only half the time.
You may know that the enemy is vulnerable to attack.
You may not know if your men are capable of attacking them.
You will still win only half the time.
You may know that the enemy is vulnerable to attack.
You may know that your men are ready to attack.
You may not know how to position yourself in the field for battle.
You will still win only half the time.

You must know how to make war.
You can then act without confusion.
You can attempt anything.

Think of your job experiences as stepping stones.
They will support you in an uncertain future.
Pick jobs with care and understanding.
They will serve you faithfully.

Some care only about their salary, not where their jobs lead.
They can love their work, but it leads nowhere.
Their job experience is spotty and unfocused.
These people spoil their future.
Their experience is useless.

You can know that your experience appeals to employers.
Nevertheless, you must know how to beat rivals.
If you don't, you have only done half of your job.
You can know how to beat rivals.
Nevertheless, you must also know that your experience will
appeal to employers.
If you don't, you have only done half of your job.
You can know how to beat rivals.
You can know how to appeal to employers.
Nevertheless, you must also know exactly how to choose
the right job situation.
If you don't, you have done only half of your job.

You must know how to select a job.
You can then act with certainty.
You can go as far as you want.

We say:
Know the enemy and know yourself.
Your victory will be painless.
Know the weather and the field.
Your victory will be complete.

We say this:
Know your rivals and your abilities.
Then success is easy.
Understand trends and organizations.
Then your success is assured.

TYPES OF TERRAIN

Use the art of war.
Know when the terrain will scatter you.
Know when the terrain will be easy.
Know when the terrain will be disputed.
Know when the terrain is open.
Know when the terrain is intersecting.
Know when the terrain is dangerous.
Know when the terrain is bad.
Know when the terrain is confined.
Know when the terrain is deadly.

Warring parties must sometimes fight inside their own
territory.
This is scattering terrain.

When you enter hostile territory, your penetration is shallow.
This is easy terrain.

Some terrain gives me an advantageous position.
However, it gives others an advantageous position as well.
This will be disputed terrain.

Career Stages

Build your career wisely.
Know when your job is tenuous.
Know when your job is easy.
Know when your job is contentious.
Know when your job is open.
Know when your job is shared.
Know when your job is serious.
Know when your job is bad.
Know when your job is limited.
Know when your job is risky.

You must sometimes defend your responsibilities against a new rival.
This is the tenuous stage of your career.

When you move into a new position, your ideas are new.
This is the easy stage of your career.

Your next possible position could be very rewarding.
Nevertheless, rivals can win this position as well.
This is the contentious stage of your career.

I can use some terrain to advance easily.
Others, however, can use it to move against me.
This is open terrain.

Everyone shares access to a given area.
The first one there can gather a larger group than anyone
else.
This is intersecting terrain.

You can penetrate deeply into hostile territory.
Then many hostile cities are behind you.
This is dangerous terrain.

There are mountain forests.
There are rugged hills.
There are marshes.
Everyone confronts these obstacles on a campaign.
They make bad terrain.

In some areas, the passage is narrow.
You are closed in as you enter and exit them.
In this type of area, a few people can attack our much larger
force.
This is confined terrain.

You can sometimes survive only if you fight quickly.
You will die if you delay.
This is deadly terrain.

You make easy progress in your job.
Rivals, however, can still come in at any time.
This is the open stage of your career.

Several people share the same responsibilities.
If you can develop good working partnerships, you will be
successful.
This is the shared stage of your career.

You have been successful in your job.
You have left many rivals in the organization behind you.
This is the serious stage of your career.

The future is difficult and unknown.
Progress is slow.
Your internal support is uncertain.
Everyone encounters such difficulties in their working life.
These are the bad stages in your career.

In some careers, there is a key transition point.
You rely on a few key relationships to get through them.
Your entire career can be undone if rivals know how dependent
you are.
These are the limited stages of your career.

Sometimes you succeed only if you take a chance.
You will fail if you delay.
This is the risky stage of your career.

To be successful, you control scattering terrain by not
fighting.
Control easy terrain by not stopping.
Control disputed terrain by not attacking.
Control open terrain by staying with the enemy's forces.
Control intersecting terrain by uniting with your allies.
Control dangerous terrain by plundering.
Control bad terrain by keeping on the move.
Control confined terrain by using surprise.
Control deadly terrain by fighting.

Go to any area that helps you in waging war.
You use it to cut off the enemy's contact between his front
and back lines.
Prevent his small parties from relying on his larger force.
Stop his strong divisions from rescuing his weak ones.
Prevent his officers from getting his men together.
Chase his soldiers apart to stop them from amassing.
Harass them to prevent their ranks from forming.

When joining battle gives you an advantage, you must do it.
When it isn't to your benefit, you must avoid it.

A daring soldier may ask:
"A large, organized enemy army and its general are coming.
What do I do to prepare for them?"

To be successful, avoid tenuous stages by not leaving openings for rivals.
During easy stages, don't stop making progress.
During contentious stages, avoid competing for jobs.
In open stages, keep up with your rivals.
In shared stages, make good alliances.
In serious stages, concentrate on generating results.
In bad stages, keep yourself productive.
In limited stages, be inventive.
In risky stages, make yourself successful.

Find the position that makes you successful.
You can use your position to cut off organizational support for your opponents.
Prevent small opposing groups from joining together.
Stop rivals from finding support from management.
Prevent rival managers from aligning their people against you.
Stop any opposition from banding together.
Pressure them to stop them from getting organized.

When fighting opposition creates an opportunity, you must fight.
When it doesn't create an opportunity, you must avoid fighting.

You may ask:
"A senior, powerful opponent is plotting against me.
 What should I do?"

Tell him:
"First seize an area that the enemy must have.
Then they will pay attention to you.
Mastering speed is the essence of war.
Take advantage of a large enemy's inability to keep up.
Use a philosophy of avoiding difficult situations.
Attack the area where he doesn't expect you."

You must use the philosophy of an invader.
Invade deeply and then concentrate your forces.
This controls your men without oppressing them.

Get your supplies from the riches of the territory.
It is sufficient to supply your whole army.

Take care of your men and do not overtax them.
Your *esprit de corps* increases your momentum.
Keep your army moving and plan for surprises.
Make it difficult for the enemy to count your forces.
Position your men where there is no place to run.
They will then face death without fleeing.
They will find a way to survive.
Your officers and men will fight to their utmost.

Military officers that are completely committed lose their fear.
When they have nowhere to run, they must stand firm.
Deep in enemy territory, they are captives.
Since they cannot escape, they will fight.

There is an answer.
You must move to a place where he cannot touch you.
He may want to damage your career.
The freedom to move is the essence of building your career.
Take advantage of a strong opponent's inability to follow you.
Your goal should be to avoid difficult positions.
Move to another position when your opponent is unprepared.

You must have the goal of making yourself an expert.
Get deeply involved in your job and focus on it.
This channels your skills without stifling them.

Use the value of your expertise to generate income.
Your expertise must be valuable enough to support your goals.

Hone your skills and don't get stretched too thin.
Use teamwork to increase your momentum.
Keep your career moving forward and plan for surprises.
Make it difficult for rivals to know who your supporters are.
Focus your efforts and don't let yourself be distracted.
Face all crises without losing your focus.
You will find a way to succeed.
Your skills and abilities will serve you well.

If you are committed to success, you lose your fear of failure.
If you are focused on your job, you can stand firm.
When you are committed, your skills are productive.
Since your expertise is needed, you will succeed.

Commit your men completely.
Without being posted, they will be on guard.
Without being asked, they will get what is needed.
Without being forced, they will be dedicated.
Without being given orders, they can be trusted.

Stop them from guessing by removing all their doubts.
Stop them from dying by giving them no place to run.

Your officers may not be rich.
Nevertheless, they still desire plunder.
They may die young.
Nevertheless, they still want to live forever.

You must order the time of attack.
Officers and men may sit and weep until their lapels are wet.
When they stand up, tears may stream down their cheeks.
Put them in a position where they cannot run.
They will show the greatest courage under fire.

Make good use of war.
This demands instant reflexes.
You must develop these instant reflexes.
Act like an ordinary mountain snake.
Someone can strike at your head.
You can then attack with your tail
Someone can strike at your tail.
You can then attack with your head.
Someone can strike at your middle.
You can then attack with both your head and tail.

Commit yourself completely to your organization.
Without being told, you must see what needs to be done.
Without being asked, you must do what is needed.
Without being pressured, you must be dedicated.
Without being watched, you must be trustworthy.

Stop any second-guessing by making your commitment clear.
Avoid failure by leaving yourself no excuses.

You may not be rich.
Nevertheless, you still want wealth.
You may fail.
It shouldn't be because you didn't commit to success.

You must be in control when you leave a position.
You may leave even when your employer begs you to stay.
While in it, you must be committed to your organization.
You should never switch jobs to avoid a problem.
You must be courageous in your career.

Make good use of a job interview.
Interviews demand quick responses.
You must practice these responses beforehand.
You should be slippery.
Potential employers will challenge your expertise.
Respond with your experience.
Potential employers challenge your experience.
Respond with your expertise.
Potential employers can challenge your dedication.
Immediately respond with your expertise and experience.

A daring soldier asks:
"Can any army imitate these instant reflexes?"
We answer:
"It can."

To command and get the most of proud people, you must
study adversity.
People work together when they are in the same boat during
a storm.
In this situation, one rescues the other just as the right hand
helps the left.

Use adversity correctly.
Tether your horses and bury your wagon's wheels.
Still, you can't depend on this alone.
An organized force is braver than lone individuals.
This is the art of organization.
Put the tough and weak together.
You must also use the terrain.

Make good use of war.
Unite your men as one.
Never let them give up.

The commander must be a military professional.
This requires confidence and detachment.
You must maintain dignity and order.
You must control what your men see and hear.
They must follow you without knowing your plans.

You may question this.
Should you prepare all your responses?
There is only one answer.
You must!

To get the most out of an interview, you must respond well
under pressure.
Remember that you and your interviewer both have a problem
to solve.
You can help each other when you both realize that you are
partners in filling a position.

Respond well under pressure.
Show your willingness to dedicate yourself to the organization.
Even this isn't enough.
Try to become a partner with your interviewer.
This is the art of collaborating.
You can solve his problems.
You must understand his organization.

Make good use of a job interview.
Put all your skills into a simple package.
Show that you are determined.

8—⚊

You must be a professional.
This requires confidence and detachment.
You must maintain your dignity and control.
You must control what a potential employer sees and hears.
Employers must believe you without knowing your plans.

You can reinvent your men's roles.
You can change your plans.
You can use your men without their understanding.

You must shift your campgrounds.
You must take detours from the ordinary routes.
You must use your men without giving them your strategy.

A commander provides what his army needs now.
You must be willing to climb high and then kick away your
ladder.
You must be able to lead your men deeply into your enemy's
territory and then find a way to create the opportunity that
you need.

You must drive men like a flock of sheep.

You must drive them to march.
You must drive them to attack.
You must never let them know where you are headed.
You must unite them into a great army.
You must then drive them against all opposition.
This is the job of a true commander.

You must adapt to the different terrain.
You must adapt to find an advantage.
You must manage your people's affections.
You must study all these skills.

You can use your experience in different ways.
You can change your goals.
You can reshape your career without planning.

You must change employers.
You must create your own promotion path.
You can use your expertise without giving your plans away.

You must provide what employers need at the moment.
You must be willing to go out on a limb and take a risk to be successful.
You must get deeply involved with your employer in finding the problems that will create the opportunities that you need to succeed.

You must motivate superiors to allow you to work.

You must inspire them to change.
You must entice them to act.
You must never let them take you for granted.
You must bring the people you work with together.
You must unite them to overcome problems.
This is the hallmark of a successful career.

You must adapt to every stage in your career.
You must adjust to your circumstances to create opportunities.
You must know how to use people's emotions.
You must learn all these skills.

Always use the philosophy of invasion.
Deep invasions concentrate your forces.
Shallow invasions scatter your forces.
When you leave your country and cross the border, you must take control.
This is always critical ground.
You can sometimes move in any direction.
This is always intersecting ground.
You can penetrate deeply into a territory.
This is always dangerous ground.
You penetrate only a little way.
This is always easy ground.
Your retreat is closed and the path ahead tight.
This is always confined ground.
There is sometimes no place to run.
This is always deadly ground.

To use scattering terrain correctly, we must inspire our men's devotion.
On easy terrain, we must keep in close communication.
On disputed terrain, we should try to hamper the enemy's progress.
On open terrain, we must carefully defend our chosen position.
On intersecting terrain, we must solidify our alliances.
On dangerous terrain, we must ensure our food supplies.
On bad terrain, we must keep advancing along the road.
On confined terrain, we must barricade a stronghold on the high ground.
On deadly terrain, we must show what we can do by killing the enemy.

Your career must be that of an expert.
Commitment to your specialty focuses your efforts.
Weak commitments dissipate your skills.
At the beginning of a commitment to a profession, you must be disciplined.
This is a critical time.
Your interests join with those of others.
You must create good partnerships.
You can dedicate yourself totally to your employer.
This is always a serious stage.
All jobs look promising when you first start them.
This is always the easy stage of a job.
Your contacts can narrow until you must rely on a few people.
This the limited stage of a career.
A career can narrow to one big decision.
This is the risky stage.

To succeed in the tenuous stage, you must show your devotion to your job.
In the easy stage, you must communicate with your employers.
At a contentious stage, you must create obstacles for your rivals.
In the open stage, you must defend your performance in comparisons with that of your rivals.
In the shared stage, you must join your partners.
In the serious stage, you must generate value.
In the bad stage, you must find another employer.
In the limited stage, you must defend your position with top people.
In the risky stage, you must prove yourself by succeeding in the challenge.

Make your men feel like an army.
Surround them and they will defend themselves.
If they cannot avoid it, they will fight.
If they are under pressure, they will obey.

Do the right thing when you don't know your different
enemies' plans.
Don't attempt to meet them.

You don't know the local mountains, forests, hills and
marshes?
Then you cannot march the army.
You don't have local guides?
You won't get any of the benefits of the terrain.

There are many factors in war.
You may lack knowledge of any one of them.
If so, it is wrong to take a nation into war.

You must be able to dominate a nation at war.
Divide a big nation before they are able to gather a large
force.
Increase your enemy's fear.
Prevent his forces from getting together and organizing.

Do the right thing and don't try to compete for outside
alliances.
You won't have to fight for authority.
Trust only yourself and your own resources.
This increases the enemy's uncertainty.
You can force one of his allies to pull out.
His whole nation can fall.

Make your job experience valuable.
If your abilities are stretched, they will develop.
When you refuse to quit, you will work hard.
When you are under pressure, you will succeed.

Ꮪ━━★

Do the right thing when you don't understand a potential employer's thinking:
Don't try to win a job from them.

You don't understand a potential employer's goals, problems, and difficulties?
Then you should not move into their organization.
You don't contact people within the organization?
You won't find opportunities there.

There is so much to know in building a career.
You must analyze every opportunity.
Otherwise, it is wrong to change jobs.

You must build your career within an organization.
A large organization has to consider the needs of a great number of people.
Increase your rivals' problems.
Prevent them from getting together and organizing.

Act correctly and don't depend upon politics within the organization.
Then you won't have to lobby for promotions.
Trust yourself and your own resources.
This decreases any rival's source of information.
You may convince your rival's supporters to abandon him.
His whole campaign may then collapse.

Distribute plunder without worrying about agreements.
Halt without the government's command.
Attack with the whole strength of your army.
Use your army as if it was a single man.

Attack with skill.
Do not discuss it.
Attack when you have an advantage.
Do not talk about the dangers.
When you can launch your army into deadly ground, even if
it stumbles, it can still survive.
You can be weakened in a deadly battle and yet be stronger
afterward.

Even a large force can fall into misfortune.
If you fall behind, however, you can still turn defeat into
victory.
You must use the skills of war.
To survive, you must adapt to your enemy's purpose.
You must stay with him no matter where he goes.
It may take a thousand miles to kill the general.
If you correctly understand him, you can find the skill to do
it.

Manage your government correctly at the start of a war.
Close your borders and tear up passports.
Block the passage of envoys.
Encourage politicians at headquarters to stay out of it.
You must use any means to put an end to politics.
Your enemy's people will leave you an opening.
You must instantly invade through it.

Give everyone credit for any success you have.
Stop what is unnecessary without being told.
Work to your utmost everyday.
Use all your skills together.

Go after new positions with skill.
Don't let anyone know.
Be aggressive when you discover an opportunity.
Don't worry about the risks.
You may lose when you try for a new position, but you can still keep your current position.
You may be discouraged by losing, but you are more likely to win a promotion afterward.

You can win many promotions and still run into problems.
If you fail to get a promotion, you can still turn initial failure into ultimate success.
You must use your skills to build your career.
To succeed, you must adapt to your organization's needs.
You must stay in sync with your organization.
It can take years and years to rise to the top.
If you understand your organization, you can find the skill to succeed.

⊶—

Do the right things at the start of a new job.
Protect your responsibilities and keep rivals out.
Don't communicate indirectly.
Give managers the confidence to let you do your job.
You must use any means to avoid internal politics.
Eventually the organization will have a better job opening.
You must instantly go for it.

Immediately seize a place that they love.
Do it quickly.
Trample any border to pursue the enemy.
Use your judgment about when to fight.

Doing the right thing at the start of war is like approaching a
woman.
Your enemy's men must open the door.
After that, you should act like a streaking rabbit.
The enemy will be unable to catch you.

Quickly win your superiors' confidence.
Waste no time.
Go beyond your duties to solve problems.
Use your best judgment about when to stand out.

Success at the start of a new job requires winning people over to your side.
You will eventually have an opportunity to move up.
When it happens, you should act quickly.
Your rivals will be unable to catch up with you.

ATTACKING WITH FIRE

There are five ways of attacking with fire.
The first is burning troops.
The second is burning supplies.
The third is burning supply transport.
The fourth is burning storehouses.
The fifth is burning camps.

To make fire, you must have the resources.
To build a fire, you must prepare the raw materials.

To attack with fire, you must be in the right season.
To start a fire, you must have the time.

Choose the right season.
The weather must be very dry.

Choose the right time.
Pick a season when the grass is as high as the side of a cart.

You can tell the proper days by the stars in the night sky.
You want days when the wind rises in the morning.

Winning a Job

There are five targets for winning a job.
The first is a person.
The second is a position.
The third is an expertise.
The fourth is an organization.
The fifth is an industry.

To go after a job, you must have the right qualifications.
To win a job, you must package your experience.

To win a job, you must go after it at the right time.
To look for a job, you must invest your time.

Choose the right time.
Potential employers must need people.

Be careful of your timing.
Pick a time when an employer can hire.

To know the right time, learn about a job before others do.
You want to pick a time when the need to hire is building.

Everyone attacks with fire.
You must create five different situations with fire and be able
to adjust to them.

You start a fire inside the enemy's camp.
Then attack the enemy's periphery.

You launch a fire attack, but the enemy remains calm.
Wait and do not attack.

The fire reaches its height.
Follow its path if you can.
If you can't follow it, stay where you are.

Spreading fires on the outside of camp can kill.
You can't always get fire inside the enemy's camp.
Take your time in spreading it.

Set the fire when the wind is at your back.
Don't attack into the wind.
Daytime winds last a long time.
Night winds fade quickly.

Every army must know how to deal with the five attacks by
fire.
Use many men to guard against them.

126

Everyone tries to win jobs.
You must be able to recognize five different hiring
situations and respond to them.

You hear about a new job within a target organization.
You make contact from the outside to find out about it.

You contact someone about a job, but there is no response.
Wait and do not appear desperate.

Wait until the organization has a formal hiring process.
Follow that process if you can.
If the process works against you, stay where you are.

Sometimes advertising your availability can help find a job.
You don't have to know of a specific opening.
Take your time putting out the word.

Look for a new job when you have had a great success.
Don't look when you have had problems.
Well-publicized successes serve you a long time.
Less visible successes are forgotten quickly.

You must master these five approaches to winning a new
job.
You must be constantly prepared to use them.

When you use fire to assist your attacks, you are being
clever.
Water can add force to an attack.
You can also use water to disrupt an enemy.
It doesn't, however, take his resources.

You win in battle by getting the opportunity to attack.
It is dangerous if you fail to study how to accomplish this
achievement.
As commander, you cannot waste your opportunities.

We say:
A wise leader plans success.
A good general studies it.
If there is little to be gained, don't act.
If there is little to win, do not use your men.
If there is no danger, don't fight.

As leader, you cannot let your anger interfere with the success
of your forces.
As commander, you cannot fight simply because you are
enraged.
Join the battle only when it is in your advantage to act.
If there is no advantage in joining a battle, stay put.

Anger can change back into happiness.
Rage can change back into joy.
A nation once destroyed cannot be brought back to life.
Dead men do not return to the living.

When you go after jobs to advance your career, you are
being smart.
Simply getting pay raises can advance your career.
Raises in pay can make your life easier.
Pay raises alone, however, don't add to your abilities.

You win jobs by discovering opportunities in the market.
It is a mistake not to concentrate your efforts on
discovering opportunities.
In building a career, you cannot waste any opportunity.

We say this:
A smart person plans his career.
A successful person studies the job market.
If a new job doesn't advance your career, don't go after it.
If it doesn't open doors, don't waste your efforts.
If your current position is still valuable, don't move.

You must never let your emotions affect your decision to
change jobs.
You must never go after a new job simply because you are
upset.
Make a job change only when it is to your advantage.
If there is no advantage in moving, stay put.

Emotions change with time.
Unhappiness in your job can turn back to pleasure.
An organization badly abandoned cannot be rejoined.
A job you leave in anger cannot be restored.

This fact must make a wise leader cautious.
A good general is on guard.

Your philosophy must be to keep the nation peaceful and the
army intact.

Knowing this, you must be careful.
A bright person is always watching.

Your goal must be to stay calm and your career going
forward.

USING SPIES

Altogether, building an army requires thousands of men.
They invade and march thousands of miles.
Whole families are destroyed.
Other families must be heavily taxed.
Every day, thousands of dollars must be spent.

Internal and external events force people to move.
They are unable to work while on the road.
They are unable to find and hold a useful job.
This affects seventy percent of thousands of families.

You can watch and guard for years.
Then a single battle can determine victory in a day.
Despite this, bureaucrats hold onto their salary money too
dearly.
They remain ignorant of the enemy's condition.
The result is cruel.

They are not leaders of men.
They are not servants of the state.
They are not masters of victory.

Your Contact Network

Building a career involves thousands of people.
It requires traveling thousands of miles.
It can destroy your family.
It will financially strain your family.
Every day, building your career is costly.

Internal and external events force people to change jobs.
They are dislocated and unable to work.
They are unable to find and hold useful jobs.
This affects their families.

You can work at your profession for years.
A single contact can determine your success in a day.
Despite all this, many people value their salary alone too
much.
They remain ignorant of what is possible.
The result is devastating.

These people are not truly successful.
They do not truly support their families.
They are not masters of their future.

You need a creative leader and a worthy commander.
You must move your troops to the right places to beat others.
You must accomplish your attack and escape unharmed.
This requires foreknowledge.
You can obtain foreknowledge.
You can't get it from demons or spirits.
You can't see it from professional experience.
You can't check it with analysis.
You can only get it from other people.
You must always know the enemy's situation.

You must use five types of spies.
You need local spies.
You need inside spies.
You need double agents.
You need doomed spies.
You need surviving spies.

You need all five types of spies.
No one must discover your methods.
You will be then able to put together a true picture.
This is the commander's most valuable resource.

You need local spies.
Get them by hiring people from the countryside.

You need inside spies.
Win them by subverting government officials.

You need double agents.
Discover enemy agents and convert them.

You must be a creative worker and a valuable manager.
You must pursue your career in the right places to succeed.
You must surpass others and know when to move on.
This requires information.
You can get this advance information.
You won't get it from astrology.
You won't get it from past experience.
You can't reason this information out.
You can only get it by asking people questions.
You must always know your job environment.

You must use five types of personal contacts.
You need contacts among your customers.
You need contacts in your organization.
You need contacts in opposing organizations.
You need contacts in the employment industry.
You need contacts in your industry's news organizations.

You must use all five types of contacts.
No one must know everything you do.
You can put together a true picture of your situation.
Information is your most valuable resource.

You need information about your organization.
Get it by winning friends among customers and clients.

You need information from within your organization.
You get it by making friends of managers and assistants.

You need information about similar organizations.
You get it by making friends in competing organizations.

You need doomed spies.
Deceive professionals into being captured.
We let them know our orders.
They then take those orders to our enemy.

You need surviving spies.
Someone must return with a report.

Your job is to build a complete army.
No relations are as intimate as they are with spies.
No rewards are too generous for spies.
No work is as secret as that of spies.

If you aren't clever and wise, you can't use spies.
If you aren't fair and just, you can't use spies.
If you can't see the tiny subtleties, you won't get the truth
from spies.

Pay attention to small, trifling details!
Spies are helpful in every area.

Spies are the first to hear information, so they must not
spread it.
Spies who give your location or talk to others must be killed
along with those to whom they have talked.

You need contacts in the employment industry.
Let them know you might be looking for a new position.
Let them know your interests.
They will take that information to competing organizations.

You need contacts in your industry's news organizations.
You must know the latest developments in the job market.

Your job is to develop a complete career.
No friendships are as important as those with your contacts.
No reward is too generous for good information.
No knowledge is as confidential as that from your friends.

You must be bright and perceptive to develop a network.
You must be open and unbiased to develop friendships.
If you aren't sensitive to subtleties, you won't find the truth
what people tell you.

You must pay close attention to small details.
Contacts are helpful in every area.

Your contacts must keep information about you
confidential.
You must cut off relationships with those who are likely to
spread the wrong information about you.

You may want to attack an army's position.
You may want to attack a certain fortification.
You may want to kill people in a certain place.
You must first know the guarding general.
You must know his left and right flanks.
You must know his hierarchy.
You must know the way in.
You must know where different people are stationed.
We must demand this information from our spies.

I want to know the enemy spies in order to convert new spies
into my men.
You find a source of information and bribe them.
You must bring them in with you.
You must obtain them as double agents and use them as your
emissaries.

Do this correctly and carefully.
You can contact both local and inside spies and obtain their
support.
Do this correctly and carefully.
You create doomed spies by deceiving professionals.
You can use them to give false information.
Do this correctly and carefully.
You must have surviving spies capable of bringing you
information at the right time.

You may want to move to another organization.
You may be interested in a certain type of work.
You may want to win a specific job.
You must first know that organization's manager.
You must know the structure of his organization.
You must know who makes the decisions.
You must know what the organization needs.
You must know who the key people are.
You must get this information from your contacts.

You want to know people in other organizations in order to win them over.
You must be willing to spend time entertaining them.
You must stay on good terms with them.
You must get them on your side and have them further your reputation.

You must do this carefully.
You need friends and supporters from throughout your own organization.
You must also do this selectively.
You can involve employment agencies without hiring them.
You don't have to be completely honest with them.
You must do this quietly as well.
You need friends who get the latest news in your industry and then contact you about it.

These are the five different types of intelligence work.
You must be certain to master them all.
You must be certain to create double agents.
You cannot afford to be too cheap in creating these double
agents.

This technique created the success of ancient emperors.
This is how they held their dynasties.

You must always be careful of your success.
Learn from the past examples.

Be a smart commander and good general.
You do this by using your best and brightest people for
spying.
This is how you achieve the greatest success.
This is how you meet the necessities of war.
The whole army's position and ability to move depends on
these spies.

There are five different types of relationships.
You must be certain to master them all.
You must have friends outside your organization.
You cannot invest too much time in developing contacts
outside your organization.

This is how people have been successful in their careers.
This is how they have risen in their industries.

You must build your career with care.
Learn from the history of past success.

You must be a good manager and a good friend.
You must know the best and brightest people as your
contacts.
This is how you achieve the greatest success.
This is how you satisfy your need for advancement.
Your current job position and your ability to change
positions depend on your contacts.

The *Art of War Plus* Series

Competor's Guides for Business and Career

Sun Tzu's The Art of War *Plus* The Art of Career Building
$14.95 160 Pages. Paperback, 5 1/2" X 8 1/2". By Gary Gagliardi.
The Art of War plus an adaptation that applies Sun Tzu's lessons to the life-long process of advancing your professional career. *The Art of War* is shown on the left-hand page; its adaptation as *The Art of Career Building* is on the right-hand page. ISBN: 1929194137.

Sun Tzu's The Art of War *Plus* The Art of Starting a Business
$14.95 160 Pages. Paperback, 5 1/2" X 8 1/2". By Gary Gagliardi.
The Art of War plus an adaptation that applies Sun Tzu's lessons to all the challenges of starting a new business in the modern marketplace. *The Art of War* is shown on the left-hand page; its adaptation as *The Art of Starting a Business* is on the right-hand page. ISBN: 1929194153.

Sun Tzu's The Art of War *Plus* The Art of Sales
$14.95 160 Pages. Paperback, 5 1/2" X 8 1/2". By Gary Gagliardi.
The Art of War plus an adaptation for sales people that applies Sun Tzu's lessons to common sales situations. *The Art of War* is shown on the left-hand page; its adaptation as *The Art of Sales* is on the right-hand page. ISBN: 1929194013.

Sun Tzu's The Art of War *Plus* The Art of Management
$14.95 160 Pages. Paperback, 5 1/2" X 8 1/2". By Gary Gagliardi.
The Art of War plus an adaptation for organization managers that applies Sun Tzu's lessons to managing people, resources, and quality in a modern organization. *The Art of War* is shown on the left-hand page; its adaptation as *The Art of Management* is on the right-hand page. ISBN: 1929194056.

Sun Tzu's The Art of War *Plus* The Art of Marketing
$14.95 160 Pages. Paperback, 5 1/2" X 8 1/2". By Gary Gagliardi.
The Art of War plus an adaptation that applies Sun Tzu's lessons to winning modern marketing warfare. *The Art of War* is shown on the left-hand page; its adaptation as *The Art of Marketing* is on the right-hand page. ISBN: 1929194021.

Competitor's Guides for Mastering Sun Tzu

Sun Tzu's The Art of War *Plus* Sun Tzu's Own Words
Translated by Gary Gagliardi. $9.95. 160 Pages. Paperback, 5 1/2. X 8 1/2..
This is the most accurate translation of the ancient classic. A character-by-character translation of the Chinese ideograms is on the left-hand pages; the corresponding English text is on the facing right-hand pages. ISBN 1929194005

Sun Tzu's The Art of War *Plus* The Amazing Secrets of Sun Tzu
by Gary Gagliardi. $14.95. 160 Pages. Paperback, 5 1/2. X 8 1/2..
The best explanation of the hidden elements in *The Art of War*. The complete text of *The Art of War* is on the left-hand pages. On the facing right-hand pages, the secrets hidden in the text are explained in words and pictures. ISBN 1929194072

Sun Tzu's The Art of War *Plus* The Warrior Class
by Gary Gagliardi. $29.95. 320 Pages. Paperback, 5 1/2. X 8 1/2..
This is a detailed discussion of each stanza of Sun Tzu's *The Art of War*. Each stanza is explained in depth for its use in modern competition. ISBN 1929194099

Competitor's Guides for Your Personal Life
(Available Summer, 2002)

Sun Tzu's The Art of War *Plus* The Art of Winning Love
by Gary Gagliardi. $14.95. 160 Pages. Paperback, 5 1/2. X 8 1/2..
The Art of War plus an adaptation for finding, winning, and holding onto a lifelong love. *The Art of War* is shown on the left-hand pages; its adaptation as *The Art of Winning Love* is on the right-hand pages. ISBN 1929194145

Sun Tzu's The Art of War *Plus* The Art of Parenting Teens
by Gary Gagliardi. $14.95. 160 Pages. Paperback, 5 1/2. X 8 1/2..
The Art of War plus an adaptation for keeping your teen alive and well until you can get them safely out of the house. *The Art of War* is shown on the left-hand pages; its adaptation as *The Art of Parenting Teenagers* is on the right-hand pages. ISBN 1929194161

More Competitor's Guides Planned!
Check www.clearbridge.com for the latest information!

Audio and Video

Amazing Secrets of Sun Tzu's The Art of War VIDEO
Plus Amazing Secrets Companion Book
$49.95. 1 1/2 Hours. VHS.   160-Page Book by Gary Gagliardi.
A video recording of a live presentation by Gary Gagliardi on the sophisticated system of competition hidden in Sun Tzu's *The Art of War*. The book, *The Art of War Plus The Amazing Secrets of Sun Tzu*, contains the complete *Art of War* text and a detailed explanation of the seminar topic, ISBN 1929194110. Video without book $39.95, ISBN 1929194080.

Amazing Secrets of Sun Tzu's The Art of War CD SET
Plus Amazing Secrets Companion Book
$39.95. 1 1/2 Hours. Set: Two CDs. 160-Page Book by Gary Gagliardi.
A recording of a live presentation by Gary Gagliardi on the sophisticated system of competition hidden in Sun Tzu The Art of War. The book, *The Art of War Plus The Amazing Secrets of Sun Tzu*, contains the complete *Art of War* text and detailed explanation of the seminar topic. ISBN 1929194129. CD Set without book $29.95, ISBN 1929194102.

Speaking and Training
Gary Gagliardi, the author of **The Art of War** *Plus* series, is available for a _limited_ number of speaking engagements. Contact Becky Wilson at Clearbridge Publishing: 206-533-9357.

Volume Discounts
All Clearbridge titles are available at a discount when purchased in quantity. Titles can be combined to qualify for discounts.

Discount Schedule

Total # of Items	Percentage Discount
5-9	15%
10-49	30%
50-99	40%
100-249	45%
250-499	46%
500-990	48%

Fax orders to Clearbridge.   FAX: 206-546-9756.

Volume Order Form

Fax to 206-546-9756

Company Name:_____

Contact Person:_____

Shipping Address:_____

City State Zip:_____

Phone Number: _____ Fax Number: _____

Quantity	ISBN	Plus Title	Retail	Total Retail
_____	1929194005	AOW & Sun Tzu's Own Words	$9.95	_____
_____	1929194013	AOW & The Art of Sales	$14.95	_____
_____	1929194021	AOW & The Art of Marketing	$14.95	_____
_____	1929194056	AOW & The Art of Management	$14.95	_____
_____	1929194072	AOW & Amazing Secrets of Sun Tzu	$14.95	_____
_____	1929194099	AOW & The Warrior Class	$29.95	_____
_____	1929194137	AOW & The Art of Career Building	$14.95	_____
_____	1929194145	AOW & The Art of Winning Love	$14.95	_____
_____	1929194153	AOW & The Art of Starting a Business	$14.95	_____
_____	1929194153	AOW & The Art of Parenting Teenagers	$14.95	_____
_____	1929194110	Amazing Secrets Video & Book	$49.95	_____
_____	1929194129	Amazing Secrets CD Set & Book	$39.95	_____

_____Total # Titles   Total Retail: $_____

Less Discount (See previous page.): $_____

Credit Card Information   Total: $_____
(Visa, MasterCard, or   Shipping charges are added to Total.
American Express only.)   Shipping is UPS Ground FOB Seattle.
Name on Card: _____

Card Address_____

City, State, Zip: _____

Credit Card Number: _____

Expiration Date: _____ Signature: _____

The Warrior Class Training Site
FREE to Clearbridge Book Owners ONLY!
On-line Training in Sun Tzu's Methods

FREE 300-Page E-Book: *The Warrior Class.* In this e-book, each stanza of *The Art of War* is explained in detail. Available on-line in Acrobat format.

FREE Slide Shows: Fourteen free slide shows, one for each chapter of *The Art of War* plus an overview. Over 300 HTML slides.

FREE Self-scoring Tests: Two tests on each chapter, one on the text and one on the concepts in *The Warrior Class* e-book.

PASSWORDS are contained in this book for accessing The Warrior Class.

Go to www.clearbridge.com/training-area.htm for the User ID and page number in this book with the current password.